The world in your kitchen

The world in your kitchen

Satarupa Banerjee

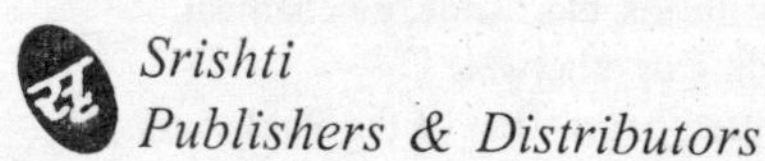

Srishti
Publishers & Distributors

SRISHTI PUBLISHERS & DISTRIBUTORS
64-A, Adhchini
Sri Aurobindo Marg
New Delhi 110 017

First published by Srishti Publishers & Distributors in 2003

ISBN 81-88575-13-5
Rs.195/-

Cover & Book design by
Creative Concept
40/223, C.R. Park
New Delhi 110 019

" The fate of a nation depends on what they eat."

Henri Brillat Savarin

Dedication

This book is for my beloved uncle
Nirmal Chandra Majumdar
Who has taught me a number of things about
continental cooking.
Many thanks Chotka.

CONTENTS

Shanghai Hilsa
Fish Mueniere
Grilled Fish With Hollandaise Sauce
Fish Florentine
Mandarin Fish

CHICKEN
67

Tomato Waldorf
Chicken Kiev
Chicken Rumaki
Moroccan Chicken Tajine
Jamaican Jerk Chicken
Chicken Mandalay
Bhuni
Chicken Roast
Chicken and Broccoli Hollandaise
Coq Au Vin
Oyako Domburi
Andalusian Chicken
Thai Chicken Red Curry
Chicken and Broccoli Gougere
Chicken Khowsuey
Fried Chicken in Lemon Sauce

MEAT
87

Crisp Crust Mutton Flan
Orange Steak
Enchiladas
Lasagne Verdi
Moussaka
Mexicalli Pancake
Rezala
Katay Masale ka Gosht

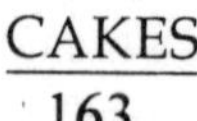

DESSERTS

MISC.

BEVARAGES

Introduction

The appearence and acceptance of international cuisines locally is a sign of globalisation. As globalisation takes root, a taste for international cuisines is now well represented in India, so much so that the choice becomes daunting. From simple hawker stalls to sophisticated, world class restaurants, international cuisines are waiting to be discovered and relished.

As the globe trotting Indian comes home after a spell he wants the taste of the world on his plate. And now Indian palates have grown in size, shape and taste with Indians increasingly becoming fond of experimenting with exotic ingredients.

To appease the growing demands of these newly discovered tastes, this book steps in.

Though Indian palate has become adventurous, one still needs to adapt the dishes to Indian tastes. I have done so wherever necessary. For instance continental cookery is mostly done with olive oil. I've used refined oil for easy availability, besides expense. But do feel free to use oilve oil.

The easy availability of foreign ingredients has made cooking with an International flair within the reach of every housewife. I hope this book will take you on a long and enjoyable gastronomic journey.

Bon Voyage.

Abbreviations

gm	-	gram
tsp	-	teaspoon
kg	-	kilogram
tbsp	-	tablespoon
lt	-	ltre
F	-	fahrenheit
ml	-	millitre
C	-	centigrade

Weights And Measures

....

Receipes in this book use the standard measuring set of cups and spoons.

A graduated set of four cups measuring one cup, a half, a third and a quarter cup.

A graduated set of 4 spoons - tablespoon, teaspoon, a half and a qurter spoon.

1 tbsp - 3 tsp 1cup - 16 tbsp.

All measurements are level unless otherwise stated.

Liquids : Place the measuring cup on a flat surface and pour the liquid to the required level. The spoons should also be filled to the level.

Dry Ingredients : These should be spooned lightly into the cup untill heaped, then levelled off with a straight edged knife or spatula. Never pack the ingredients down or shake or tap the cup. And unless specified, measure before shifting.

Moist Ingredients : It is these ingredients, like shortening and brown sugar, that have to be packed in tightly. Press the fat into the cup so that air spaces are forced out level fat to straight edge when full.

Glossary

Condiments And Nuts

English	Hindi
All spice	Kababchini
Aniseed	Saunf
Arrowroot	Araroht
Asafoetida	Hing
Baking powder	Khane ka soda
Bay leaf	Tejpatta
Black pepper or peppercorns	Kali mirch
Breadcrumbs	Sukhi double roti ka choora.
Caraway seeds	Shahjeera
Cardamoms	Elaichi
Cashewnuts	Kaju
Cinnamon	Dalchini
Cloves	Laung
Coconut, desiccated	Sukha nariel ka choora
Coconut, fresh	Nariel
Coriander leaves	Hara dhania
Coriander seeds	Sookha Dhania
Cumin	Jeera
Curry leaves	Curry patta/ meetha neem ke patte
Dry pomegranate seeds	Anardana, Sookhi
Feunel	Saunf
Fenugreek	Methi/Kasuri Methi
Garlic	Lasan
Ginger, fresh	Adrak
Ginger, dry	South
Green chillies	Hari Mirch
Jaggery (molasses)	Gur
Groundnuts	Moongphalli
Lemon rind	Nimbu ka chilka

Mace	Javitri
Mango powder	Amchur
Melon seeds	Magaj
Mint leaves	Pudina
Mustard seeds	Sarson or rai
Nutmeg	Jaiphal
Onion seeds	Kalonji
Pistachio	Pista
Poppy seeds	Khus khus
Raisins	Kishmish
Red chillies	Lal mirch
Saffron	Zafran/Kesar
Sesame seed	Til
Star Anise	Chakriphool
Sultanas	Munakka
Tamarind	Iurli
Turmeric	Haldi
Thymol Seeds	Ajwain
Vinegar	Sirka
Vetivier	Kewra

<u>Fruits</u>

Apples	Seb
Apricots	Khubani
Banana	Kela
Fig	Anjen
Grapes	Angoor
Lemon	Meetha Nimbu
Lime	Nimbu
Mango	Aam
Orange	Narangi or Santra
Peaches	Aadoo
Pears	Nashpati
Pineapple	Anaras
Pomegranate	Anar
Papaya	Papita

Sweet Lime	Musambi

Vegetables

Beetroot	Chukandar
Brinjal (Egg plant, aubergine)	Baingan
Cabbage	Band Gobhi
Capsicum	Shimla Mirch
Carrot	Gajar
Cauliflower	Phool Gobhi
Cucumber	kheera
Fenugreek Leaves	Methi ke patte
French Beans	Phras bean
Green peas	Matar
Mushrooms	Gucchi
Onions	Pyaz
Potatoes	Aloo
Pumpkin	Kaddu
Spinach	Palak
Spring Onions	Hara pyaz
Tomato	Tamatar
Turnip	Shalgam
White Gourd	Lauki

Lentils And Cereals

Bengal gram	Chana dal
Black gram	Udad dal
Corn	Makkai
Flour	Maida
Wholemeal flour	Atta
Green gram	Moong dal
Gram flour	Besan
Large White Gram	Kabuli chana
Lentil	Masur dal
Red gram	Arhar dal
Rice	Chawal
Sago	Sabudana

Semolina	Suji
Wheat	Gehu
Cracked wheat	Dalia
Puffed rice	Murmura
Pressed rice	Chiwda or Poha

<u>Cooking Terms</u>

Baking	:	Cooking by dry heat in an oven.
Barbecue	:	To roast either whole or cut pieces of any meat on direct heat on a spit or rack. Ofcourse, fish or any veg etable can also be barbecured.
Basting	:	Pouring spoonfuls of melted far over the surface of food being baked or roasted.
Batter	:	Mixing of flour, gram flour, cornflour with water, milk or any other liquid into a thin consistency.
Beating	:	An up and down motion with a fork or rotary beater to mix the food thor oughly and to introduce air.
Binding	:	Adding egg, cream or melted fat to a dry mixture to hold it together.
Bite Size	:	Small pieces of food that can be eaten in one bite.
Blanching	:	Removing the outer skin by plunging in hot water and then in cold water eg. blanching of almonds or tomatoes.
Blending	:	Mixing of two or more ingredients into

a smooth paste.

Boiling	:	Cooking in liquid at a temperature of 100 ^{0}C.
Boning	:	Removing bones of meat, poultry or fish.
Bread	:	To cover with fresh or dry breadcrumbs completely.
Browning	:	Searing the outer surface of meat to seal in the juices.
Brushing	:	Applying an even coating of milk, egg or butter on the surface of foodto get a shiny top.
Caramelize	:	To cook sugar till it turns golden.
Chilling	:	Cooking food without freezing, in the refrigerator.
Chop	:	To cut food into small pieces with a knife or blender.
Coat	:	To sprinkle food with, or dip it into flour etc., until completely covered.
Colander	:	Perforated metal or plastic basket used for draining liquid.
Combine	:	To mix ingredients.
Creaming	:	Mixing two or more ingredients with a wooden spoon or mixer to make them soft and creamy.
Cube	:	To cut food into small cubes (about 1 cm)
Dice	:	To cut into small pieces.
Dot	:	To place small blobs of fat over the surface of food.
Dough	:	A mixture of flour, water or milk, which is firm enough to knead and form into shapes.
Drain	:	To remove liquid from solid food.
Dress	:	(a) To arrange or garnish food. (b) To

pluck, draw and truss a chicken or poultry.

Dressing : A sauce used for pouring on salad before serving.

Dusting : Sprinkling lightly with salt, pepper, flour, sugar or spices.

Fillet : Long, thin boneless piece of meat or fish.

Flake : Separate food gently with a fork (like flaking fish from bones).

Folding in : Mixing one ingredient into another, normally with a spatula.

Frying : Cooking food in a little fat in an open pan is called shallow frying. Deep fry ing is cooking by immersion in a deep pan of hot fat.

Garnish : Decorating a dish with something edible that adds colour and flavour.

Grate : To rub against a grater to get this shreds.

Gravy : The resultant liquid that is left after cooking food.

Grilling : Cooking directly oven an open flame, generally on high heat.

Julienne : Vegetables cut in thin match like strips.

Karahi : A heavy iron pan for deep frying. Nowadays steel aluminium or non-stick karahis are also available.

Knead : To work dough with hands, pressing, stretching and folding until it is smooth.

Marinate : To coat or soak food with certain spices or sauces for a period of time. This helps infuse flavours or, as in the case of meats, to tenderise them.

The combination of spices or sauce is called marinade.

Melt	:	To heat and liquify.
Mince	:	To chop food very fine.
Paanch phoran	:	A mixure of nigella, mustard, cumin, fenugreek and aniseeds used in Bengali cooking.
Parboil	:	To partially boil food.
Pare	:	To peel the outer covering.
Poach	:	To cook egg by placing it shelled in boiling water. Or, to cook food in a sim mering liquid.
Puree	:	To press food through a fine sieve or blend in a blender to make a smooth paste.
Pot Roast	:	Cooking large pieces of meat or poul try by braising.
Pressure Cook	:	Is to drive out all the air, and thus have a very high temperature in which the food cooks, so that it is much faster. It is important to read the instructions of your pressure cooker, before use.
Prove	:	To let a dough rise till double in vol ume, in case of dough made with yeast.
Rest	:	Is literally to rest a dough for a certain period of time. A term mostly used for doughs or batters.
Rinds of Lemons	:	Are generally used to add zest to a dish. It is only the outer coloured or Oranges portion of the skin of the fruit that is used.
Roast	:	To cook by dry heat in an oven or on an open flame.
Rub in	:	Flour and fat are mixed together by rubbing with the fingertips to re

semble fire breadcrumbs.

Saute : To fry food rapidly in hot fat and toss ing and turning often.

Scald : Means (a) cooking in a liquid, just be low boiling point. This temperature is indicated when tiny bubbles form around the edge of the pan. (b) Dip ping food in boiling water.

Sear : To brown the surface of food quickly over high hear (generally meat).

Season : To add whole spices into hot fat so the fat is impregnated with the flavour of the spices. An important step in In dian Cooking.

Seasonings : Herbs and condiments used to im prove the taste and appearance of food.

Sift : To pass through a sieve.

Simmering : To cook gently over low heat.

Skewer : Long metal or wooden thick pins used to pierce meat or fish for keeping them in place during roasting.

Skillet : A heavy shallow frying pan with slightly raised Sides.

Steaming : Cooking in a double boiler or in a ba sin standing in (but not covered by) boiling water.

Steeping : Soaking in liquid to remove an ingre dient e.g. salt from dried fish.

Stirring : Mixing in a circular motion.

Stock : Liquid in which meat, poultry or fish is cooked.

Tarka : To garnish food with herbs and con diments by frying in hot fat to enrich its taste and flavour.

Temper : Same as to season.

Toast	:	To cook food over dry heat or under a grill to make it brown and crisp.
Toss	:	To mix foods lightly with a lifting mo tion, using two forks or spoons.
Trivet	:	The perforated plate used in a pres sure cooker through which stream passes.
Truss	:	To fasten wings etc., of fowl with thread before roasting.
Whip	:	To beat rapidly with fork, mixer or egg beaten to introduce air so that volume is increased.
Whisk	:	To stir or beat very briskly; a hand or electric beater or wire whisk is used.
Yeast	:	This is the raiser for bread dough. There are generally two types of yeast, fresh or compressed and dry.
Zest	:	Grated outer skin of fruit which is used to flavour foods and liquids.

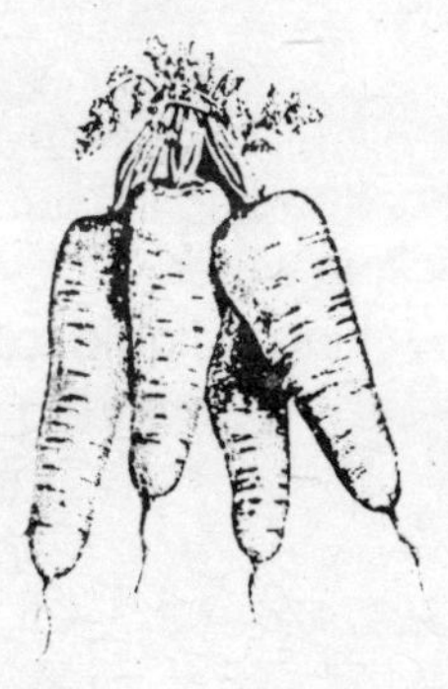

Soups

Mushroom And Walnut Soup

Take your pick of the soup and ward off winter chill.

Ingredients

2 tbsp chopped walnuts, 1½ tbsp butter
1 medium onion, finely chopped, 100 gm mushrooms, chopped
900 ml chicken stock, 1 tsp grated nutmeg
Salt and pepper to taste, 6 tbsp cream
chopped spring onion, walnuts for garnishing

Soak the walnuts in boiling water for 5 minutes; drain.

Heat the butter in a saucepan. Saute the onions till soft and transparent. Add the mushrooms and fry 2 minutes. Add the stock, nutmeg, salt and pepper. Cook for 15 minutes on high heat.

Blend the walnuts to a paste in the processor. Add the soup and blend till smooth. You will have to do it in batches.

Reheat and serve garnished with spring onions and walnuts.

Can be served chilled too.

Serves 6.

Chilled Fruit Soup (Israel)

Iced delight for the hot and bothered.

Ingredients

500 gm plums, 250 gm pears, 1 large tin cherries, 1/4 cup sugar, 1/4tsp salt, 1 tsp cinnamon powder, grated rind and juice of 1 lime, 5 cups of water, 1 tsp cornflour.

Stone and halve the plums. Peel core and halve pears, chop coarsely. Dessed the cherries.

Place all the fruits in a large saucepan. Add the sugar, salt, cinnamon, lime juice and rind. Pour in the water and bring to boil over high heat, stirring occasionally. Reduce heat to low, cover and cook the fruits for 15 minutes or till very tender. Alternatively pressure cook with 4 cups of water for 10 minutes.

Remove pan from the heat. Blend to a puree and strain. Return syrup to the pan. In a small bowl, mix the cornflour with 2 tbsp of the soup. Add gradually, stirring all the time. Bring to the boil, stirring constantly.

Reduce heat to moderate and cook for a further 5 minutes or until thickened slightly. Taste and add more sugar, if needed.

Remove and let cool to room temparature. Refrigerate to chill for at least a couple of hours before serving, garnish with mint sprigs.

Prawn And Lychee Soup

Stop a minute, taste this; life is good.

Ingredients

500 gm lychees, 300 gm prawns, 1 tsp refined oil, 1 medium onion, chopped fine. 1 tbsp grated ginger, 1 cup tomato puree, 1 tsp sugar, salt and pepper to taste. 1/2 cup cream, 1/4 cup slivered almonds, 1 tsp lime juice, 4 cups stock.

Peel the lychees, discarding the stones.
Peel and devein the prawns, discarding heads.

Heat the oil in a saucepan. Saute onion and garlic till soft. Add 1 cup stock, puree, prawns, sugar, salt and pepper. Cook over a low heat till the prawns are cooked. Save a few prawns for garnishing and blend the rest of the soup till smooth.

Combine the soup, remaining stock and cream and pour into a saucepan, stirring until well mixed; cook over low heat until heated through.

Add the lychees, almonds and lime juice check seasoning. Heat through and serve garnished with prawns.

Serves 6.

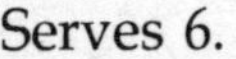

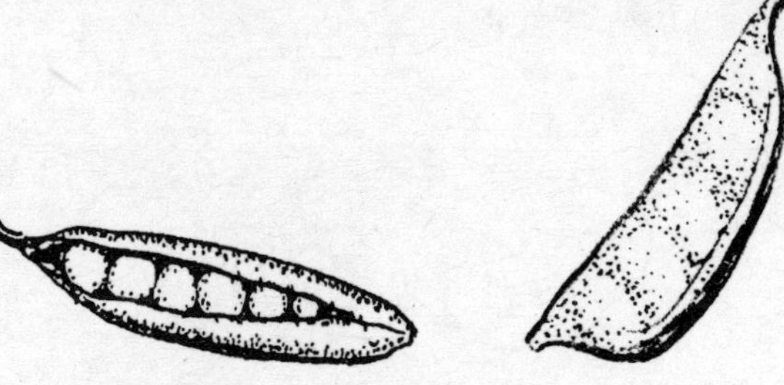

Tom Yam Kai (Thai Chicken Soup)

Thai hot and sour chicken soup that's gently spiced exhales the aroma of lemon grass and kafir lime leaves. This is a soup to be enjoyed at a leisurely pace allowing the spiees and heat of the surprisingly light base to slowly warm you up and gently prepare the palate for the main course.

Ingredients

8 cups chicken stock, 2 slices of ginger,
2 stalks lemon grass, 2 cups thinly shredded chicken,
3 tbsp fish sauce, 2 lime leaves, bruised. 1 green chilli, crushed.
Salt to taste, 2 tbsp lime juice, 2 tbsp fresh coriander.

Grind to a paste : 1 clove garlic. 3 peppercorns.
2 tbsp choped fresh coriander.

Bring 4 cups of the stock to the boil. Add the ground paste. Stir well. When it comes to a boil again add ginger slices, chopped lemon grass (white part only) and shredded chicken Cook. Covered till the chicken is done.

Add the remaining stock, fish sauce, lime leaves, crushed green chilli and salt. Cook for 5 minutes on low heat, uncovered.

Add the lime juice and fresh coriander.

Stir once and serve hot.

Serves 4.

Bouillabaisse

This is a classic french soup to write home about.

Ingredients

800 gm mixed white fish fillet, 3 tbsp refined oil.
2 medium onions, Sliced. 6-8 unshelled green peas,
2 tomatoes, chopped. 12 cloves of garlic, chopped.
pinch of saffron. Salt and pepper to taste. 1 bay leaf.
1.2 lt water. 250 gm shelled prawns, 150 ml white wine
(optional). 1 cup toasted croutons dash of chilli sauce.

The fish should be cut into small pieces. By white fish I mean pomfret, bhetki, mackarel, morh etc.

Heat the oil, add the onions, garlic, peas and tomatoes. Fry gently until soft. Add the fish, saffron (mixed with 1 tbsp water), salt pepper, bay leaf and chilli sauce. Fry for a minute and add the water.

Cook for 10 minutes, stirring occasionally. Add the prawn and wine, if using. Let boil for another 10 minutes. Remove from heat and discard bay leaf.

Pour the soup into a tureen adding a handful of chopped parsley and croutons as garnish.

Serve 6.

Prawn Bisque (France)

There are still many parts of the continent, where soup, perhaps alongside a loaf of bread and a jug of wine is synonymous with the word 'food'. This pink, thickish soup is so delicious and satisfying that you can easily get addicted to it.

Ingredients

6 cups chicken stock, 2 cups shelled and deveined prawns,
3 tbsp butter, 1 tbsp sunflower oil, 2 large onions, finely chopped.
2 bay leaves, 1 stalk parsley, 1 large carrot, minced.
½ cup finely chopped celery.
1/3 c finely chopped leek, (white part only), 5 peppercorns,
1 cup fresh tomato puree, 1½ tbsp rice, 2 tsp brandy.
Salt and pepper to taste.

You may prepare the stock with the prawn shells. Boil a few prawns and keep aside for garnishing.

Heat the butter and oil together in a saucepan, prefrably a nonstick one, saute the onion till translucent. Add the bay leaf, parsley stalk, carrot, celery, leek and peppercorn and prawns. Lower heat and saute for 5 minutes.

Add the tomato puree. 4 cups stock and rice. Bring to a boil. Add the brandy. Salt and pepper. cover and simmer till the rice is done. Remove the bay leaf and parsley.

When cool enough to handle, blend in mixie. Reheat alongwith the rest of the stock. Serve garnished with cream and boiled prawns.

Salads

Mango Prawn Cocktail

A piquant variation of an old gavourite. Serve this starter with melba toasts.

Ingredients

1 large ripe mango, 200 gm prawns. 2 hard boiled eggs, 1 tbsp mango chutney, 4 tbsp mayonnaise, 1/4 tsp capsico sauce, 1 tsp worcestershire sauce, 1 tsp lime juice, 1 tsp powdered sugar, Salt and pepper to taste, 1 small bunch of lettuce.

The mango must not be overripe. Peel and dice small. Shell and devein prawns. Cook in very little water till they turn pink. Drain.

Shell and roughly chop the eggs. If they mango chutney has chunky pieces in it, chop them roughly.

Combine the mayonnaise, capsicum, tomatoes, lime juice, sugar, salt, pepper and mango chutney. Stir in the prawns. Let stand for an hour for the flavours to mingle. Stir the eggs and mango pieces gently into the prawn mixture.

Shred the lettuce finely and divide equally between 4 large wine glasses. Spoon the prawn mix over the lettuce just before serving; lettuce becomes linp with standing. Serve with melba toast.

Melba Toast : Trim the crusts of 4-6 thick bread slices. Roll with a rolling pin till thin. Cut into triangles.

Toast the breads. Watch carefully while its under the grill as it curls and the corners may burn.

Serve in a napkin lined basket to keep warm.

These toasts keep well for a week, at least in an airtight container.

Serves 4.

Kokonda

An African spicy fish salad. Goes well with any menu. Serve with bread.

Ingredients

750 gm boneless thick fish fillets, 7 tbsp lime juice, 1 green capsicum, 1 red capsicum. 2 small cucumbers, 2 large tomatoes, 3 large bananas. 1/2 cup black grapes, 1/2 cup green grapes, 1/2 cup grated coconut, 1 tbsp finely chopped parsley.

Dressing: 1/2 cup thick curd, 1/2 cup whipped cream, 1 tsp salt, 1 tsp freshly ground pepper, 1/2 tsp roasted and powdered cumin, 2 finely chopped green chillis.

Cut the fish in small cubes. Lightly fry the fish till done. Or, you may steam fish, if you don't want to use oil marinate fish in lime juice for an hour.

Deseed and chop capsicum into very small pieces. Peel and dice cucumbers. Chop tomatoes. Peel and dice bananas. The grapes can be kept whole or halved.

Drain fish from the lime juice. Mix fish with all salad ingredients in a large bowl. Sprinkle parsley all over.

iv) Mix all the dressing ingredients together and pour over the salad. Chill for an hour before serving.

v) Serves 6.

German Potato Salad

Germany, alongwith Ireland and Russia, is one of the great consumer of potatoes. Potatoes have been given a raw deal over the years - rumour has it, they're fattening. But in fact, a large 200 gm potato has 220 calories and less than one gram of fat what's more, they're a good source of complex carbohydrates, vitamins and minerals.

Ingredients

3 eggs, 4 cubes cheese, 300 gm potatoes, 3/4 cup mayonnaise, 2 tbsp finely chopped onion, 2 tbsp finely chopped green capsicum, 2 tbsp finely chopped red capsicum, 1/4 cup sweet chutney, Salt and pepper to taste, 1 tsp malt vinegar, Lettuce leaves.

Hardboil the eggs and chop coarsely. Dice the cheese cubes. Cook the potatoes till done. Peel and dice small.

While the potatoes are still hot, mix with the mayonnaise. This helps the potatoes to absorb the flavour better.

In a bowl, combine the potatoes, cheese and eggs. Toss lightly to combine.

In another bowl, mix the onion, green and red capsicum, sweet chutney, salt, pepper and vinegar.

Pour over the potato mixture. Toss lightly to coat well. Cover and chill.

Line a salad bowl with crisp lettuce. Serve the salad over the lettuce.

Serves 4.

Moulded Tuna Salad

To unmould a chilled salad, dip the mould for a few seconds in warm water and invert on a plate. The moulded salad will slide easily.

Ingredients

1 large tin tuna, 1 tbsp gelatine, One and half cup strong chicken stock, 1/2 cup mayonnaise 3 cups chopped boiled eggs, ½ cup green grapes, ½ cup black grapes, ½ cup chopped celery, 3/4 cup cooked peas, lettuce leaves, tomato slices and more grapes for garnishing.

Drain the fish and cut into small pieces.

Soak the gelatine in 1/2 cup stock for 15 minutes or till spongy. Bring the remaining stock to boil. Add the gelatine and stir till dissolved. Chill till thick like unbeaten egg white.

Add the mayonnaise, eggs, grapes, celery, peas and tuna.

Lightly oil a mould and pour in the salad. Chill till set.

Unmould on a lettuce lined plate, garnished with grapes and tomato slices.

Serves 6

Guacamole

Actually a mexican dish, but finds place in many a continental menus. Try with an Indian meal, you won't be disappointed.

Ingredients

2 ripe avocados. 1 tbsp lime juice 1 small onion grated. 2 cloves garlic, crushed. 1 green chilli, very finely chopped. 1/3 cup chopped fresh coriander, salt and freshly ground pepper to taste.

This needs well ripened avocados that mash easily. Halve the avocados and remove stones. Scoop out flesh with the help of a spoon. Place in a bowl, drizzle with lime juice at once to prevent discolouration. Mash till smooth.

Add the remaining ingredients. Stir well and cover. Chill for an hour before serving.

Serves 4.

Achara Salad (Fish Salad from Philippines)

The cuisine of the Philippines offers an 'oriental Latin' flavour which is unique, not only in Asia, but throughout the world which in itself, by its very spice and variety is a reflection of the people who make up this vibrant archipelago.

Ingredients

500 gm boneless fish cubes, 200 ml malt vinegar.
2 tbsp lime juice.1 small onion. 1 red capsicum.
1 green capsicum. 1 cm piece ginger. peppercorns.
Salt and white pepper to taste. Oil for frying fish.

The fish should be cut into bite sized pieces. Soak fish in vinegar for 2 hours. Remove fish and squeeze away excess vinegar and saute in hot oil till done. Remove.

Finely chop the onion, capsicums and ginger, crush the pepper corns. Add to the fish, pour the lime juice, salt and pepper. Mix well and serve.

Serves 4

Cooked Chinese Salad

Stir frying is the most commonly used method of chinese cooking. Food is cut into small pieces and fried quickly over high heat using just a little oil. Here the same principle is put to good use for a cooked hot salad.

Ingredients

4 spring onions. 1 large red capsicum. 1 large green capsicum.
250 gm carrots. 125 gm french beans.2 tbsp refined oil.
2 cups bean sprouts. 1 cup shredded cabbage.
Fried noodles for garnishing.

Dressing : 1 tbsp light soya sauce. 2 tsp sweet chilli sauce. 1 tbsp brown sugar. 1 tbsp malt vinegar. Pinch monosodium glutamate. Salt and pepper to taste.

Thinly slice the spring onions diagonally. Cut capsicum and carrot into/juliennes and french beans into strips.

Combine the dressing ingredients and keep aside.

Heat the oil in a Karahi till it is really hot. Swirl it around. Add the spring onions, beans and carrots; stir fry for 2 minutes. Add the capsicums, cabbage and bean sprouts and stir fry for another 2 minutes.

Add the dressing and stir fry for 2 minutes more making sure all the vegetables are coated with the sauce.

Place over a serving dish. Sprinkle fried, noodles and serve at once.

To deep fry noodles : Break noodles into small pieces. Boil for 2 minutes. Do not overcook, strain and sprinkle a lilt flour.

Heat enough oil in a Karahi for deep frying. Add the noodles and fry till crisp. Take out and drain on absorbent paper.

Serves 6

Som Tam

Generally som tam or Thai papaya salad is made with raw papaya. Its amazingly good. This is slightly different - 'it uses ripe papaya. Its excellent.

Ingredients

2 medium ripe papayas or 1 large, ½ cup shredded cabbage.
1 small head lettuce, 2 tomatoes, ¼ cup roasted peanuts,
2 spring onions, sliced thinly, white part only
fresh basil to garnish.

Dressings : 4 tbsp refined oil, 1 tbsp fish sauce or light soya sauce, 2 tbsp lime juice, 1 tbsp grated jaggery or a palm sugar, 1 tsp finely chopped green chilli or to taste, 1 tbsp coconut cream.

Choose ripe but firm papaya. Peel and discard seeds. Cut into pieces. Take only the inner white part of the cabbage and shred finely. Shred the lettuce.

Blanch the tomatoes. To do this cover the tomatoes with boiling water and leave for 2 minutes. Take out and peel. Remove the Seeds and chop the flesh.

Arrange the lettuce and cabbage on a plate. Mix the tomato and papaya lightly and place over the leaves. Scatter the peanuts and spring onion all over.

Whisk the dressing and pour over the salad. Garnish with fresh basil.

Dressing: whisk together the oil, fish sauce or soya sauce, lime juice, jaggery or palm sugar and chillis. Stir to dessolve sugar and use as directed.

Serves 4

Pasta

Pasticcio

Pasta's popularity has always been its adaptibility. It can come in many different forms with taste differences and visual variety. It can be a meal in itself like the following or eaten with other foods, too.

Ingredients

For the macaroni : 250 gm elbow macaroni. ½ tsp salt, 2 eggs, slightly beaten, 4 tbsp cream. ½ cup grated cheese.

For the sauce : 1 red capsicum, cored, seeded and chopped. 2 cloves garlic, chopped. 600 gm boneless chicken, chopped coarsely 400 gm balnched, peeled, seeded and chopped tomatoes. 1 cup chicken stock. 1 tbsp malt vinegar. Salt and pepper to taste. 2 tbsp chopped parsley. Dash of ground cinnamon, cloves and all spice, each. 2 tbsp refined oil. 1 onion, thinly sliced.

For the topping : 300 ml curd, 3 eggs, freshly grated nutmeg. ½ cup grated cheese. Salt and pepper to taste.

To cook the macaroni : Cook the macaroni in a pan of boiling salted water till just done. Drain and mix with the eggs, cream and salt. Set aside.

To make the sauce : Heat the oil in frying pan and fry the onion and capsicum for 3 minutes. Add the garlic and cook for 1 minute. Add the mince and cook till browned.

Add the tomatoes, stock, vinegar, salt, pepper, and ground spices; bring to the boil. Simmer for 20 minutes, until thickened. Stir in parsley and remove.

To make the topping : Beat the curd and eggs together and season with nutmeg, salt and pepper. Stir in the cheese.

The finale : Spoon half the macaroni mixture into a greased baking dish. Sprinkle half the cheese.

Place all of the meat sauce on top. Pour remaining macaroni. Then pour all the topping over the macaroni. Sprinkle the rest of the cheese.

Bake in preheated 350 ^{0} F / 180 ^{0} C oven for 45 minutes.

Serve hot.

Family Pasta Medley

Pasta is fast gaining a reputation as a wonderfully nutritious food in India. And it is so economical that pasta deserves to be served oftener.
To cook pasta correctly, just bear the following points in mind.

Heat ample water to cook pasta. You may add salt and a little oil to the water. The more water, the less likely it is that the pasta will stick together. Water should come to a fast boil.

Add pasta to the rapidly boiling water gradually, so that the water continues to boil. Cook, uncovered, stirring occasionally to keep the pasta from sticking together or sticking to the bottom of the pan, especially during the first minute of cooking time.

Do not overcook pasta. Test for doneness by pressing a piece of pasta against the side of the pan with a fork or a spoon; pasta will break easily and cleanly when done. Or test by tasting; properly cooked pasta is firm to the bite, or "al dente". If pasta is to be baked or cooked further in a recipe, undercook it somewhat.

Drain pasta thoroughly in a large colander. Do not rinse pasta unless it is being used in a salad.

One and half cups thinly sliced carrots. 1 cup thinly sliced celery. ½ cup chopped onion. 1 tsp minced garlic. 2 tbsp olive or refined oil.

3 cups cubed cooked boneless chicken or prawns. 1 cup blanched and seeded tomatoes, chopped. 1and 1/3 cups pasta sauce. 1 cup apple juice. ¼ cup chopped parsley. ½ tsp dried basil. ½ tsp salt. 1 tsp freshly ground pepper. 3 cups uncooked spiral pasta.

For the pasta sauce : 9 large tomatoes. 2 tbsp Olive or refined oil. 2 bay leaves. 5 peppercorns. 1 small onion, chopped. 1 tsp minced garlic. 1 small capsicum, halved and salt to taste. 4 tsp sugar. ½ tsp dried oregano.

Heat the oil in a Saucepan. Sante the carrots, celery, onion and garlic till soft but not brown. Stir in the remaining ingredients except the pasta. Simmer, uncovered for 20 - 25 minutes to blend flavours.

In the meantime, cook the pasta and drain. Toss with the hot sauce and serve.

To make the pasta sauce : Blanch the tomatoes in boiling water. Peel, deseed and finely chop.

Heat the oil in a Saucepan. Add the bay leaves and peppercorns and Sante for a few seconds. Add the onion, garlic and capsicum and sante for 5 minutes.

Add the tomatoes and let simmer for 15 minutes. Add salt and sugar and cook, stirring continually till quite thick finally add the oregano and mix well. Remove the capsicum, bay leaves and peppercorns and use as directed.

Refrigerated, this sauce keeps well for at least a week.

Pasta Almondine

Ingredients

Almonds and raisins lend a crunchy. Richness to this sauce.
2 tbsp butter. 650 gm chunky fish fillets. 300 gm penne pasta.
2 egg yolks, beaten.

For the almond sauce : 100 gm butter, 3 tbsp flour. ¼ tsp grated nutmeg, Salt and white pepper to taste, 1 cup stock, 1/3 cup raisins, 15 Sultanas (munakka), ¼ cup blanched and slivered almonds, 1 tbsp lime juice, 1 tsp sugar.

Cook the pasta till just done. Strain and reserve.

Melt the butter in a frying pan and gently saute the fish until cooked through. You'll have to do it in batches. keep aside.

To make the almond sauce : Melt the butter in a skillet and stir in the flour; cook, stiring until the roux is smooth and golden. Add nutmeg, salt and white pepper and cook briefly. Gradually pour in the stock, stirring continuously.

When the sauce is smooth, stir in the raisins, sultanas, almonds, lime juice and sugar. Bring to the boil and simmer over low heat for 10 minutes.

Whisk a little of the hot stock into the egg yolks, then with the saucepan off the heat, whisk the egg yolk mixture back into the sauce. Stir to mix. Keep warm.

Place pasta in a serving plate. Top with fish pieces, than pour on the sauce.

Serves 4

Szechuan Noodles

This somewhat spicy dish is enlivened by chilli oil. The egg, meat, vegetable and natural flavourings make a nourishing combination which can be varied as desired.

Ingredients

For the chilli oil : 1 cup groundnut oil. 1 cm piece of ginger, crushed. 2 tbsp red chilli powder.
Heat the oil in a pan. Do not let it smoke. Remove from heat. Add the crushed ginger. Stir. Add the chilli powder. Stir. Set aside half an hour to cool. Strain the oil through a thick cloth. Store in a bottle. This oil will keep for at least a couple of months at room temperature. It will last longer in the refrigerator. 6 tbsp chilli oil. 2 pkts. boiled noodles. 1 tbsp grated garlic. 2 large onions, chopped. 3 dry red chillis. 2 cups shredded cabbage. ½ cup each shredded beans. Carrots, capsicum, spring onion. ½ cup cooked chicken, diced ½ cup cooked prawns. 6 tbsp soya sauce. 1 tbsp chilli sauce. ½ tsp monosodium glutamate. 1 egg. 1 tbsp tomato sauce (optional).

Heat 2 tbsp chilli oil and just toss the noodles so that they are thinly coated with the oil. Remove and set aside.

Heat 4 tbsp chilli oil and lightly fry garlic, onion and dry red chillis, broken in pieces. Now, add the carrots and beans. Fry for 5 minutes. Side in the noodles. Toss to coat and heat through.

Make a thin omlette with the egg. Roll and cut into strips. Garnish with the egg strips and shredded spring onions.

Serves 4

Pasta With Chicken And Pineapple Sauce (Italy)

Ingredients

1 large chicken, about 1.2 kg, 1 large onion grated, 6 cloves of garlic, grated, 1 egg, ½ cup breadcrumbs refined oil for frying, 1 tbsp cornflour. Salt to taste. 1 tsp paprika powder, Pinch of mustard pd, ¾ cup tomato ketchup, ¾ cup tomato puree, 2 cups cooked pasta, 4 tbsp cooked peas, parsley for garnishing.

Joint the chicken in regular pieces and cook in 2½ cups of water with salt, grated onion and chopped garlic. Remove chicken when done. Reserve the stock. If you're using a pressure cooker, use less water.

Deep the chicken pieces in the beaten egg, roll in breadcrumbs and fry in hot oil till a light brown. Keep aside.

Sauce : Combine the stock, cornflour, salt, paprika, mustard pd. Tomato ketchup and puree. Cook over a medium heat till thick. Mix pineapple pieces and remove.

Cook the pasta till 'at dente' - that is it should still have a bile left in it any small shaped pasta will do.

To serve : Place the fried chicken in the centre of a plate. Surround with the pasta and place clusters of peas all around. Pour sauce on top of the chicken and garnish with parsley leaves.

Bami Goreng : (Fried noodles from Indonesia)

This dish of Indonesian origin is popular all over the far east. The mixture of chicken, prawn and meat gives this dish a delightful succulence that is similar to the spanish dish of paella, only this one uses noodles.

Ingredients

300 gm noodles, 2 spring onions, 2 cloves garlic, 4 green chillis, 5 tbsp refined oil, 1 cup shelled and deveined prawns, 100 gm cooked, shredded chicken, 100 gm cooked, shredded meat, 3 tbsp light soyabean sauce, 1 tbsp fish sauce, Salt and white pepper to taste, 3 eggs.

Place the noodles in a saucepan of rapidly boiling water. Add 1 tsp oil and salt, each. Add the noodles and cook for 3 minutes. Drain throughly.

Grind the spring onion, garlic, green chilli with 1 tbsp oil to a smooth paste.

Heat the remaining oil in a pan. Add the paste and stir fry for 3-4 minutes. Stir in the prawns, chicken, meat and season with soya sauce, fish sauce, salt and freshly ground white pepper.

Cook over a moderate heat for 5 minutes till the prawns are done.

Add the beaten eggs and cook, stirring continuously until the eggs begin to set. Finally add the noodles, stir to blend throughly. Serve immediately.

Serves 4.

Rice

Butter Rice and Chicken

Ingredients

For the rice : 250 gm basmati rice, 4 tbsp butter, 1 medium carrot, 50 gm French beans, ½ cup cooked peas. 2 pinches dried rosemary, 1 tbsp finely chopped parsley, Salt and pepper to taste.

For the chicken sauce : 2 tbsp butter, 3 tbsp flour, 1½ cups milk, pinch rosemary, 1½ cups cooked and shredded chicken, 1 cup chicken stock, Salt and pepper to taste.

For the rice : Cook rice till half done, Strain. Finely chop the carrot and beans.

Heat the butter in a saucepan. Add the carrot, beans and peas. Stir fry for 5 minutes. Add the preboiled rice, rosemary, parsley, salt and pepper, sprinkle 2 tbsp water; cover and cook till rice is just done. All the grains should remain separate.

Remove onto a bowl. Press and level surface. Keep hot.

For the chicken sauce : Heat the butter in the same saucepan. Try flour till cream coloured. Reduce heat and add the milk, stirring constantly. Cook over a moderate heat, stirring continually till thick. Add rosemary, salt and pepper. Add the chicken and stock. Cook for 5 minutes till. Quite thick. Remove.

To serve : Turn the bowl of rice onto a platter, pour the sauce over.

Garnish with cherries, mashed potatoes, and boiled and santeed vegetables. This makes a full meal.

Serves 2

Thai Green Fried Rice

Instead of serving dishes in courses, a Thai meal is served all at once so that diners can enjoy complimentary combinations of different tastes.

Ingredients

850 gm cooked rice. 100 ml refined oil, 150 gm onions, finely chopped, 4 cloves garlic, Finely chopped, 1 tsp sugar, 1 tbsp heaped green curry paste, 2 cups prawns, cooked. 3 eggs, lightly beaten, 1 tsp chilli sauce, 2 tbsp fish sauce, 1 capsicum, diced, 1 cup cooked peas. 2 tbsp beans, diced. 2 tbsp spring onion, chopped, 2 tbsp gresh coriander for garnishing, salt to taste.

For the green curry paste : 15 green chillis, 4 stalks spring onions, 1 tbsp grated ginger, 1 tbsp garlic, 2 lime leaves, 1 tsp lime rind, 4 stalks lemon grass (white part only`, 1 tbsp roasted coriander seeds, 1 tbsp roasted cuminseeds, 4 tbsp fresh coriander, 3 tbsp refined oil. - grind all together.

Heat the oil in a large kadhai, saute the onion and garlic till soft. Add the sugar, salt and curry paste and stir - fry for 2 minutes.

Stir in the prawns and mix well to coat with the chilli paste. Push to one side of the kadhai, away from the centre. Add a little more oil, if required and pour in the beaten eggs. Lightly scramble.

Add the rice, breaking lumps, if any; stir until heated through. Add the chilli sauce, fish sauce, capsicum, peas, beans and spring onion, stir frying after each addition. Cook till are the ingredients are well mixed and the vegetables are crisp linder.

Remove and serve hot.

Serves 4

Iranian Polo

'Polo' in Iranian means pulao. It is the name applied to rice when its mixed with other ingredients in the cooking process. The Iranians consider 'Polo' as the essence of an exquisite dinner.

Ingredients

100 gm dried aprocots. 400 gm basmati rice. 100 gm ghee, 1 large onion. Finely chopped. 1 tsp cuminseeds. 2 bay leaves, 6 green cardamoms, 12 peppercorns. 1 tsp turmeric. 1 tsp cumin powder. Salt to taste, 4 cups chicken stock or water. ½ cup whole cashewnuts, ½ cup blanched almonds. 1/3 cup shelled pistachios, ½ cup raisins, 100 gm seeded and chopped dates. 1 tbsp sugar, ½ cup black grapes. ½ cup green grapes, 1 cup red pomegranate seeds.

Wash and soak apricots for 2 hours. Discard the seeds and dice. Wash and soak the rice for 1 hour. Drain.

Heat the ghee in a heavy based degchi. Temper with the bay leaves. Cuminseeds, cardamoms and peppercorn. When they turn a shade darker, add the onions. Cook, stirring, for 2 - 3 minutes until softened. Add the turmeric and cumin powder and stir for half a minute.

Stir in the rice and stir for 3 - 4 minutes till the rice turn opaque. Add the heated stock or water, salt and sugar. Bring to boil. Add all the dry fruits, stirring once. Cover and reduce heat.

When the liquid is almost absorbed and holes appear on the surface, keep a tawa underneath the degchi and cook for 20 - 25 minutes. Gently stir with a fork and serve at once garnished with grapes and pomegranate seeds.

Delicious with a meat curry or a kabab.

Serves 6

Jambalaya

A classic example of Cajun cooking. Cajun food is the new taste sensation from America. The Cajuns are the descendants of the French settlers called Acadians who came from Canada in the 1750's. Their cooking was influenced by the spices, herbs, seafood and vegetables they found when they migrated down the Missisipi.

Ingredients

2 tbsp butter. 2 tbsp refined oil. 1 large onion, finely chopped. 1 tsp minced garlic. 2 capsicums, cored and diced. 1 stick celery, diced. 2 cups cooked, boneless chicken cubes. 1 cup shelled prawns. 1 chicken stock cube, crushed. 1 cup cooked peas. 1 tsp Capsico sauce. 2 tsp worcestershire sauce. ½ tsp dried thyme. ¼ tsp dried oregano. ½ tsp white pepper. ½ tsp freshly crushed pepper. ¼ tsp paprika, 400 gm basmati rice. 700 ml chicken stock. Salt to taste.

Heat the butter and oil together in a large degchi. Add the onion and garlic. Saute till soft, but not brown. Add the capsicum and celery, cook, stirring continually for 3 minutes.

Add the chicken and prawn and cook further for 2 - 3 minutes. Stir in the crumbled stock cube, capsico sauce, Worcestershire sauce, herbs spices and salt. Stir well for a couple of minutes.

Stir in the rice and saute for 2 minutes. Add the stock, heated. Bring to boil, cover and reduce heat.When the water is almost absorbed, stir with a light hand and put a tawa underneath the degchi. Cook for another 20 minutes or until the rice is done and dry.

Variation : Use ham and sausages; or omit non-vegetarian ingredients use only vegetables. Add cauliflower, broccoli, beans, carrots.

Serves 6

Yakhni Pulao (Bangladesh)

Yakhni means stock. Pulao cooked in yakhni definitely tastes better. Biriani may be more well known, but it is the yakhni pulao which is cooked more in Bangladesh, oftener than any other rice classic.

Ingredients

200 gm curd. 1½ kg meat. 4 tbsp refined oil. 1 tsp aniseeds. 15 peppercorns. 4 black cardamoms. 4 bay leaves. 1 dry red chill. Salt to taste. 1 tsp sugar, a handful of raisins. 2 tbsp ghee. 1 tbsp caraway seeds. 4 cloves. 4 cinnamon sticks. 4 green cardamoms. 10 peppercorns. 4 bay leaves. 4 green chillis, chopped. 2 tsp ginger paste. 1 kg basmati rice. 4 tbsp butter. 1 cup chopped coriander leaves. 1 cup milk.

Grind together : 2 large onions. 2 cm ginger. 5 cloves garlic. 4 green chillis.

Beat the curd and marinate meat in it for one hour. Heat the oil and temper with aniseeds, peppercorns, black cardamoms, dry red chillis and ground paste and fry for 5 minutes.

Add the meat, salt, sugar and raisins and fry for another 5 minutes. Add 8 cups of hot water and pressure cook for 10 minutes. Strain and reserve stock. Discard the spices as much as possible.

Heat the ghee in a degchi and temper with caraway seeds, garam masala, peppercorns, bay leaves and green chillis. When you get a fried aroma, add the ginger paste and stir for 30 seconds. Add the rice and fry till opaque. Remove.

Lightly grease a rice cooker. Layer 1/3 rice half the meat, followed by 1/3 rice, rest of the meat and top with the remaining rice. Add a little butter and coriander leaves on each layer. Finally sprinkle the remaining butter and coriander leaves on top.

Pour the milk and stock (this should measure 8 cups) over the rice gently close cooker and cook till done.

This can be cooked in a degchi the same way. But in that cause use 7 cups of stock only. Finish over dum.

Serves 8 - 10.

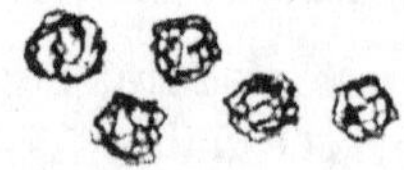

Congee Rice

Congee rice is a chinese standby, equally popular at breakfast, midday or evening. Served with pickled vegetables, it becomes a full, meal. Very light and easily digested, congee can be safely served to children and old people, too.

Ingredients

8 cups of water. 225 gm chicken. 1 cup rice. 1½ tsp salt.
½ cup shelled peas. 225 gm spinach or lettuce, chopped.
1 tbsp light soya sauce. 2 tsp ginger juice, pepper powder to taste.

Bring the 8 cups of water to a boil; put in the chicken and cook until well done, removing any scum which forms. Strain the stock and chop the cooked chicken in small pieces.

Put the stock, rice, salt and peas to boil, partially covered. Reduce heat when it comes to a boil and cook for 40 minutes. Congee must be cooked slowly. Add the chicken during the last 10 minutes. Now add the spinach or lettuce, ginger juice, soya sauce and pepper. Cook for another 10 minutes. The mixture should resemble a thick soup.

Serve hot in soup bowls. Fish, chicken or mutton liver can be used instead.

Serves 4

Kedgree

Kedree comes from the Hindi word 'khichree'. It used to be breakfast food in England. Now, it is served any time of the day. I find it a most successful brunch dish.

Ingredients

100 gm butter. 3½ cups cooked rice. 1 tsp curry pd. 1½ cups cooked prawns. ½ cup fried fish fingers. ¾ cup fried surmai cubes. 4 hardboiled eggs, quartered. 300 ml cream. 2 tbsp chopped spring onion. Salt and pepper to taste. 1 tbsp Worcestershire sauce.

Heat the butter in a large heavy based saucepan. Stir in the rice and curry powder and cook over a low heat till heated through.

Stir in the prawns, both kinds of fish. Cover and leave over a very low heat until hot.

Stir in the eggs, cream, spring onion and Worcestershire sauce. Taste and add salt and pepper. Serve immediately.

Serves 6

Risotto Novara (Italy)

Risotto is actually Italian khichdi. There are as many ways of preparing risotto as there are families in Italy. The Italians use arborio rice, which is small grained. In Calcutta, I use 'gulab-swarup' quite successfully. But any rice can be used if small grained ones are not available.

Ingredients

350 gm rice. 1 kg fresh green peas or 350 gm frozen peas. 4 tbsp butter. 2 tbsp groundnut oil. 1 cup shelled and deveined prawns. 1 small onion, sliced. 1 spring parsley, finely chopped. 1½ lt. Stock salt and pepper to taste, grated cheese.

Wash and drain the rice. Shell the peas, if using fresh ones.

Heat half the butter and oil in a saucepan, non-stick preferred, and saute the prawns, onion and parsley for 2-3 minutes. Add the peas and cook for another couple of minutes. Add the rice and cook until transluscent.

Heat the stock and add to the rice 125 ml at a time, stirring constantly and making sure the liquid has been absorbed before adding more. After about 10 minutes, stir in the salt and pepper. The risotto is done when the rice grains are tender, yet still firm to bite.

Remove the pan from the heat and stir in the grated cheese and the remaining butter. Serve at once.

Variation : Use chicken, mince, ham, bacon or any other vegetable of your choice.

How to prepare mascaporne cheese at Home. Put 300 ml cream and heat over very low heat till kukewarm. Add a pinch of tartaric acid (or you can use a tbsp of curd). Stir till incorporated; then keep covered in a warm place till set. Refrigerate for 8-10 hours. Then line a bowl with heavy cheesecloth, pour in the mixture, allow the whey to drain out and refrigerate until ready to use.

Breads

Probably the most appetising aroma is that of freshly baked breads. Contrary to many housewive's belief, baking bread is not difficult at all. It may be somewhat time consuming, but you can do other jobs while the dough is rising. And I can assure you the taste of a fresh home baked bread is worth all the time and labour.

There are three stages to making bread;

1. Mixing the bread in correct proportions to prepare the dough.

2. Using leavening agents (yeast) to aerate the dough.

3. Baking the leavened dough.

The main ingredients are flour, water, yeast and salt.

Flour - Any type of flour or a combination of flour can be used. Flour proteins combine with water to form gluten. Gluten's extensible properties help in the development of the dough.

Water helps in gluten formation. It dessolves the salt and sugar and helps distribute the yeast cells through the dough.

Yeast is a lining organisation. You can buy fresh yeast in frozen state, but it has to be brought to the room temperature to activate it. Yeast is the leavening agent, when the tiny yeast plants feed on sugar, they produce carbon dioxide gas which makes the dough rise.

Pita Bread (Middle East)

Pita breads are very much in vouge these days. It is of Middle Eastern origin. It may be split in half for filling with small pieces of meat, paneer, vegetables and salads. It may also be served as accompaniment of dips.

Ingredients

1 tbsp fresh yeast. ½ tsp sugar. 300 ml warm water.
450 gm flour. 1 tsp salt.

Stir the yeast into the warm water alongwith the sugar. Cover and let ferment for 5 minutes.

Sift the flour and salt together and mix to a dough with the yeast liquid. Knead throughly on a lightly floured board for about 10 minutes until the dough is smooth, elastic and non sticky. Keep the dough in a greased bowl. Cover and prove in a warm and drought free place until double in size, approximately 1 hour.

Knock back the dough. Knead well again. Divide into 8 pieces. Roll each portion into an oval shape 25 cm x 13 cm. Put on greased baking trays. Cover with oiled polythene sheets and set aside to rest for 10 - 15 minutes. Bake in an oven preheated to 220° c / 440° f for 6-8 minutes. Do not overbrown. Wrap the pitas in a clean, damp tea towel to cool to make them soft and pliable. Can be reheated and served.

Steamed Bun (China)

Chinese in origin, these steamed buns are a treat.
A refreshing change from baked buns.

Ingredients

Dough : 1½ tsp fresh yeast. 1 tsp sugar. ¾ cup milk. 2 cups flour. 1 tbsp oil. ½ tsp salt.

Filling : 100 gm fresh mushrooms. 2 tbsp sunflower oil. 2 medium onions, finely chopped. 1 tsp finely chopped ginger. 1 tsp finely chopped garlic. 1 green chilli, finely chopped. 50 gm paneer, grated. Salt to taste.

Masala paste grind together - ½ tsp cuminseeds. ½ tsp coriander seeds. 1 dry red chilli or 5 peppercorns. 1 blade of mace a pinch of garam masala powder.

Wash and finely chop mushrooms. Heat the oil. Add the onions. When these pick up brown spots, add ginger, garlic and green chillis. Stir fry. Add the masala paste and fry well. Add the mushroom and salt. The mushroom will release a lot of water. When the moisture evaporates a little add the paneer and fry well. Let the moisture evaporate completely. Remove. Divide into 12 portions.

Prepare a bread dough as per the recipe of milk bread. Knead well after the first rising and divide into 12 portions. Stuff each portion of the dough with one part of the stuffing. Let rise for 15 minutes.

Roll into smooth buns. Steam them for approximately 10 minutes. You'll have to do this in batches. Steam in a momo steamer. Or, boil water in a degchi; put a colander over it and place the buns on it. Cover and steam.

Serve the buns with mushroom sauce.

Brown Bread

Brown bread is a lot more healthy than white bread.

Ingredients

250 ml milk. 1 tbsp fresh yeast. 30 ml lukewarm water.
3 tbsp honey or treacle. 1½ tsp salt. 2 tbsp groundnut oil or butter.
300 gm whole wheat flour (atta).

Mix the yeast with the lukewarm water. Keep covered for 10 minutes.

Heat the milk to the boiling point; add the honey or treacle and stir well. Let cool till lukewarm.

Sieve the flour and salt together. Rub in the oil or butter. Add the yeast ferment to the lukewarm milk and knead the dough with it. Proceed as for the milk bread recipe, kneading very well after the first rising.

Bake in a loaf tin. Remove from the tin and cool the loaf. Slice and serve.

Ingredients

1 tbsp fresh yeast. ½ cup tepid water. 2 tbsp powdered sugar.
250 gm flour. 2 tbsp butter or margarine. 1/4 tsp salt. 1 egg.
50 gm tutti fruitti. 25 gm raisins.

Add the yeast to the water with a pinch of sugar and 1 tsp flour. Cover and let ferment for 5 minutes.

Beat the egg and sugar lightly. Sift the flour and salt together. Rub in the butter or margarine. Make a bay in the centre and add the fermented yeast mixture. Mix. Now add the egg mixture and knead to a soft dough. Put in an oiled bowl and cover. Let rise till double in volume about 1 hour.

Turn dough out on to a lightly floured board and allow it to rest 10 minutes cover with wax paper to prevent drying. Knead the dough until it is smooth and satiny about 10 minutes or until it springs back when pressed with fingers. To knead, fold the dough over on itself. With the lower part of your palms, push the dough with two or three strokes; turn the dough one qurter away around on the board, fold it over again, and repeat the kneading until the dough is smooth. Now, add the dry fruits. Mix well.

Divide into 10 - 12 equal portions. Shape into smooth round balls. Place on greased tray and keep for final proving till double in size again. Brush with beaten egg. Make a light cross mark on each bun and sprinkle with sugar.

Bake in an oven preheated to 400°F / 200° c for 15 - 20 minutes or till done. Take out and brush with melted fat and sugar syrup.

Garlic Bread

You can buy fresh yeast in blocks. Keep in freezen compartment of your refrigerator wrapped in cleing filen and then keep in an airtight container. Will keep for 6 - 8 months, at least.

Ingredients

1 tbsp fresh yeast. 1 tsp sugar. ¾ cup tepid water. 1½ cups flour.
½ cup dry milk powder. 1 tsp salt. 2 tbsp butter or oil.
1 whole pod of garlic, ground.

Sift the flour, milk powder and salt together. Ferment the yeast with the sugar and tepid water.

Rub the oil into the flour. Add the ground garlic and then the yeast. prepare a soft dough. Knead a little and keep covered in an oiled bowl for aprx. 1 hour or till double in volume. Keep in a warm and drought free place.

Take out, punch the dough to remove all gas and knead well stretching and folding to incorporate air. When smooth and elastic, shape and keep in an well oiled loaf tin for the final proving till double in size, aprx. 20 - 25 minutes. Do not touch the dough at this stage.

Bake in an oven preheated to 400° F / 200°c for about 30 minutes.

Salt gives taste to the dough. It should always be sifted with the flour. If added straight, it slows down the action of the yeast.

The bread is done when it. Shrinks from the pan or if the loaf sounds hollow when you tap it with your knuckles. The bread should be removed immediately from the oven and placed on the cooking rack. These can then be brushed with butter.

Croissant (France)

These crescent shaped bread rolls are indeed as much a part of the French Cuisine as roast beef and Yorkshire pudding are part of an English menu.

Ingredients

300 gm flour. 175 gm butter. 1 tbsp sugar. ¾ tsp salt.
1 tbsp fresh yeast. 1 cup milk.

Ferment the yeast in lukewarm milk and sugar for 5 minutes.

Sift the flour with the salt and rub in 25 gm of the butter. Refrigerate the remaining butter.

Prepare a soft dough with the flour and yeast mixture. Knead well for 4-5 minutes and let prove in a covered bowl for 50 minutes or until doubled in bulk.

Knead once again and roll out the dough on a lightly floured surface to a rectangle. 18 cm x 25 cm approximately. Cut the cold butter into thin slices and spread two thirds of it over the middle section of the dough. Brush the edges of the dough with water.

Fold the two slides of the dough to the middle and press the outside edges firmly together to seal. Spread the rest of the butter on the right side and brush water over the edges. Fold the left side over the right and press the edges down to seal.

Turn the dough round lengthwise; roll it out and repeat the folding process without the butter. Let it rest for 10 minutes in the refrigerater and then roll it out again. Repeat the folding and rolling process two more times. Refrigerate for half an hour.

Roll the dough to a rectangle 1.25 cm thick and cut into 15 cm squares. Cut each square into triangles. Roll the triangle from the broad end to the tip finishing with the tip underneath.

Curve these into crescents and place on oiled trays. Brush with beaten egg. Cover and let rise for 15 minutes. Bake in an oven preheated to 400° F / 200°c for 15 -20 minutes.

You can prepare croissant sandwiches by cutting the roll in half and puting any filling of your choice.

Pumpkin Scones

Savoury scones are perfect accompaniments to soups, stews and casseroles as well as being delicious with tea or coffee.

Ingredients

3 tbsp butter. 2 tbsp brown sugar. ½ cup mashed, cooked pumpkin. 1 egg, beaten. ½ cup milk. 2½ cups flour. 2 tsp baking powder. Pinch salt. ½ cup raisins. Melted butter to glaze.

Cream the butter and sugar, then mix in the pumpkin. Stir in the egg and milk.

Sift the flour baking powder and salt together. add to the butter mixture with the raisins. Knead a few times on a lightly floured surface, then pat out to a rectangle about 2 cm thick.

Cut into rounds with a cutter or into squares with a sharp knife. Brush tops with melted butter.

Bake in a preheated 200°c / 400°F oven for 15 minutes, until well risen, golden on top and cooked through.

Serve hot, split and buttered - with honey also, if liked.

Fish

Fish Normandy

Extremely simple and incredibly quick to put together.

Ingredients

For the pastry : 250 gm flour. ½ tsp salt pinch of pepper. 100 gm buter. 150 ml refined oil. 2 egg yolks. 1 tbsp lime juice. 4 tbsp cold water.

For the filling : 500 gm cooked and flaked fish. 2 cups handboiled eggs, chopped. 1 tbsp parsley. 1 apple cored, peeled and chopped. 300 ml thick white sauce. 1 egg yolk. 1½ tsp lime juice. Pinch pepper. 2 dashes capsico sauce.

For the white sauce : 50 gm butter. 50 gm flour. 250 ml milk. Salt and pepper to taste. (Make sauce according to basic recipe).

To make the pastry : Sift the flour with salt and pepper into a mixing bowl. Add the butter and oil and mix with your fingertips till it resembles coarse breadcrumbs.

Beat the egg yolks; mix the lime juice and water. stir into the flour and mix with a light hand till a soft and pliable dough is formed. Do not overknead or use a heavy hand.

Divide into 2 unequal portions and roll out on a floured surface.

Take an 10 inch (25 cm) pie dish and cover the dish with the larger crust, up the sides as well. Trim the excess. Spoon the filling into the dish until reasonably full. Place the remaining of the rolled pastry dough across the top tacking down the sides. Brush the upper crust with milk or beaten egg yolk. Prick at a few places so steam can escape.

Bake at 220 ° C / 450 ° F for 10 minutes. Then reduce heat and bake at 190 ° C /380 ° F for 20 minutes. The milk on the top crust ensures that it turns a deed golden.

To make the filling : Mix all the ingredients together gently and fold into the white sauce.

Daab Chingri (Prawns in coconut)

This is a rather exotic dish from Bangladesh. Traditionally it was cooked in coal embers. But baking is easier. Ask your coconut vendor to remove the outer husk of the green coconut as much as possible. This shortens the cooking process and enables the coconut to fit in the oven.

Ingredients

1 medium green coconut. ½ kg. prawns. 1½ tbsp mustard paste. ½ tsp turmeric. 4 green chillis. Salt to taste. 1 tbsp mustard oil.

See to it that the green coconut has some tender meat in it. Cut a portion off the top of the coconut (the coconut seller will do it for you). Remove the cut portion. Shell and devein the prawns. Discard the coconut water.

Mix the prawns, mustard paste, turmeric, salt and slit green chillis. Put this inside the coconut. Fix the top portion with atta dough.

Bake it in an oven preheated to 200 ° C / 400 ° F for 45 - 50 minutes.

Let cool slightly; break open the top and take out the prawns alongwith the coconut meat and serve hot with plain boiled rice.

Serves 6

Fish Pasanda

Bangladesh, being a land with many rivers, thrives on fish. Fish has such wonderful attributes that it is highly regarded throughout the world.

Ingredients

8 pieces large, but thin fish fillets juice of 1 lime. 2 eggs. Salt and pepper to taste. 100 gm cornflour or flour, refined oil for frying. ½ tsp baking powder.

For the stuffing : 1 tbsp refined oil. ¾ cup shelled and defined prawns. 1 small onion, finely chopped. 2 tbsp chopped cashewnuts. 1 tbsp raisins. 1 tsp grated ginger. Salt to taste. 2 tbsp fresh coriander. 1 tsp desiccated coconut. ½ tsp roasted and powdered cumin. ¼ tsp garam masala powder. ½ tsp sugar.

For the gravy : 2 tbsp refined oil. 1 cup groun onion. 1 tsp ginger paste. 1 tsp garlic paste. 1 tsp green chilli paste. ½ tsp turmeric. ½ cup tomato puree. 2 tbsp ground fresh coconut. 1 tsp sugar. Salt to taste.

Soak the fish fillets in water mixed with lime juice for 15 minutes. Drain and dry with paper towel.

Prepare a batter with the beaten eggs, salt pepper, cornflour or flour and baking powder. Add the flour gradually till you get a batter of coating consistency.

Divide the stuffing in 8 equal parts and place one portion on to each part. Roll from one end. Press well on all sides to seal.

Dip in batter and deep fry in oil till golden. Remove and keep aside.

Stuffing : Heat the oil and fry the onions till soft. Add the remaining ingredients and fry till the prawns are done.

Gravy : Heat the oil in a karahi. Fry the ground onions till pink. Add ginger, garlic, green chilli paste and fry till the raw smell of the garlic disappears.

Add the turmeric, puree, ground coconut, sugar and salt. Stir for another 2 minutes. Add 1½ cups of water and let cook for 10 minutes on high heat till gravy thickens and oil floats on top.

Pour the gravy over the fish pasandas and serve hot.

The pasandas can be eaten as a snack, too.

Serves 4 - 6.

Fish With Dill

Fish to taste right, should swin 3 times; in water in butter and in wine - polish proverb.

Ingredients

2 cups chopped carrot, leek and celery combined. 1 onion, chopped. 15 peppercorns. 4 bay leaves. 4 tbsp white wine. Salt to taste. 4 large, thick bhetki fillets. 1 lime, halved. 1 tbsp butter, 1 tbsp flour. 1 tsp sugar. ½ cup cream. ½ cup dill.

Accompaniments : 2 tbsp butter. 500 gm baby corn, broccoli, red and green capsicum, mushrooms, beans all combined. 2 large potatoes, boiled with a pinch of saffron, 1 cup milk. Salt and pepper to taste.

Cook all the vegetables and onion in 1½ cups of water, peppercorns, bay leaves, white wine and salt for 25 minutes or till well done. Add lime halves and fish and cook covered for 5 - 7 minutes. Take out the fish; strain stock and discard the vegetables.

Melt the butter in a frying pan and fry the flour. Take off heat a add the stock, stirring constantly. Put on heat and stir well. Add cream, salt sugar and dill. Let cook on low heat for 1 minute.

Accompaniments : Parboil broceoli, mushroom, beans all diced. Heat butter and saute them for 2 - 3 minutes. Add sliced baby corns, capsicum, salt and pepper. Toss and cook for 5 minutes.

Cook the potatoes with milk, saffron, salt and pepper. When done, strain and toss potatoes in butter.

To serve : Place the fish in a platter. Surround with vegetables and potatoes. Pour the sauce on top. Garnish with dill.

Serves 4.

Sarmali (stuffed vine leaves) (Turkey)

Since vine leaves are not easily available, use cabbage leaves instead.
12 medium cabbage leaves. 1 cup chicken stock. 1/3 cup chopped parsley. 1 tbsp refined oil. 4 tomatoes cut in wedges for garnishing.
Stuffing : 250 gm fish. 1 tbsp refined oil. 2 large onions, finely chopped salt and pepper to taste. 2 tbsp finely chopped parsley. 2 tbsp tomato ketchup. 1 cup cooked rice.
Blanch the cabbage leaves. Drain and leave on a tray to cool.

Divide the stuffing into 12 portions. Wrap one portion in each cabbage leaf. Roll up like a parcel to form a sausage like shape.

Lay them in a baking dish. Cover with the stock. Sprinkle parsley and oil.

Bake in an oven preheated to 200 ° C / 400 ° F for 20 minutes. Serve hot garnished with tomato wedges.

Stuffing : Boil and flake fish, discarding the bones.

Heat the oil in a frying pan; add the onions and fry till soft and translucent. Add the rest of the ingredients and mix well. Remove and use as directed.

Minced meat may be used in place of fish.

Serves 6.

Tuna Potato Scallop

Ingredients

300 gm potatoes. 200 gm tinned tuna. 2 tbsp butter.
2 tbsp flour. Salt and pepper to taste. 350 ml. milk.

Topping : 125 ml mayonnaise. 1 tbsp worcestershire sauce a pinch of chilli pd. a generous pinch of mustard pd.
½ cup grated cheese.

Mayonnaise : 1 egg yolk. 1 tsp lime juice. 1 tsp vinegar.
150 ml refined oil. ½ tsp salt. ½ tsp sugar. ¼ tsp mustard pd.
Boil, peel and cut potatoes in thick rounds. Drain tuna.
Break into large pieces.

Melt butter in a saucepan. Fry flour till the raw smell disappears, but it must not brown. Add milk gradually. Stirring well. Add salt and pepper and cook till glossy, smooth and thick. Add tuna; mix well.

Grease a baking dish, arrange potatoes and tuna mix in

alternate layers, beginning and ending with the potatoes. Mix together mayonnaise, worcetershire sauce, chilli pd. mustard and grated cheese, spread over the potatoes. Bake in an oven preheated to 350 ° F / 180 ° C for 40 minutes. Serve hot.

Mayonnaise : All the ingredients should be at room temparature. Beat the egg yolk in a bowl. Add the lime juice and vinegar and beat again. Add the oil, one drop at a time, beating continuously when it emulsifies add 1 tsp oil at a time and beat till thick. Add the seasonings. Beat well to mix.

Serves 4

Prawn With Peas

A simple and tasty dish from szechuan.

Ingredients

12 large prawns. 2 tbsp rice wine or sherry. ½ tsp salt.
1 tsp ginger juice. 1 1/3 cup shelled peas, cooked, 2 green chillis.
1 clove garlic. A small piece of ginger. 2 tbsp groundnut oil.

For the sauce : 2 tbsp sugar. 2 tbsp rice wine, 2½ tbsp soya sauce.
2 tbsp tomato ketchup. ½ cup of water.

Shell and devein the prawns. Marinate with the wine, salt and ginger juice. Remove the seeds from the green chillis and chop finely with the garlic and ginger.

Mix the sauce ingredients together throughly in a bowl, making sure that the sugar dissolves completely.

Heat the oil in a karahi. Add the drained prawn. Stir fry until the prawns change colour; add the green chilli, ginger and garlic. Stir fry for 1 minute and set aside.

In the same oil. Stir fry the peas. When the peas are coated with oil, return the shrimp to the pan, pour in the sauce and mix well. Serve hot.

Serves 4

Shanghai Hilsa

You don't have to be a bengali or a cat to enjoy hilsa. This king of fish has a flavour that's unique and cannot be matched by any other. The bones are so soft and thin that they can be easily managed.

Ingredients

500 gm hilsa, cut into pieces. 4 tbsp oil. 3 tbsp gin. 10 cm piece of ginger. 15-20 cloves garlic. 4 tbsp light soya sauce. 1 cup shredded spring onion.

Scrape and cut the ginger into large pieces. Crush the ginger and garlic lightly.

Take a pan that will hold the fish in a single layer. Pour all the ingredients except spring onion, over the fish. Steam for 10 - 15 minutes. Garnish with the spring onion and serve.

Serves 4

Fish Mueniere (France)

Ingredients

500 gm thick fish fillets. Salt to taste. Juice of 2 limes. 1 tbsp capsico sauce. 1 tbsp worcestershire sauce. 1 tbsp tomato ketchup. 2 tbsp flour. White pepper to taste. 100 ml groundnut oil. 60 gm butter. ¼ cup finely chopped parsley, fried potato fingers and grapes for garnishing.

Soak the fillets in water mixed with 1 tsp salt and juice of 1 lime for 5 minutes. Wash well and pat dry.

Marinate the fillets in a mixture of capsicum, worcestershine and tomato sauce for half an hour.

Season the flour with salt and white pepper. Drain the fish. Coat lightly with the seasoned flour.

Heat the oil in a skillet till smoking. Remove from the fire and put in the fish. Fry over a medium heat on both the sides till done and a light golden.

Place the fried fish in an oval dish neatly. Keep the firely chopped parsley in the centre. Garnish with the potato fingers and halved grapes by the sides.

Melt the butter and pour over the parsley. The butter will start to foam and look very pretty. Do this on the dining table in from of your guests serve each fried fish with a little of this butter sauce.

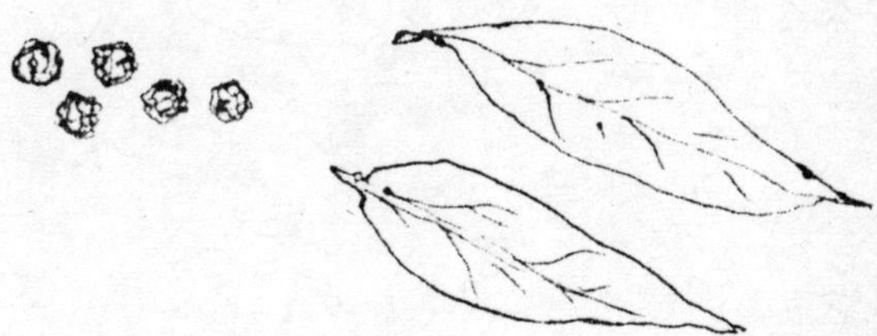

Grilled Fish With Hollandaise Sauce
(England)

Once you have mastered the technique of a good Hollandaise sauce, you're on your way to becoming an excellent cook.

Ingredients

750 gm thick fish fillets. 1½ tbsp flour. Salt and white pepper to taste. 75 gm butter, melted, juice of 1 lime.

For the Hollandaise sauce : 2 tbsp malt vinegar. 5 peppercorns. 4 tbsp water. 3 egg yolks. 175 gm butter at room temparature. Salt and white pepper to taste, a few chops of lime juice.

Brush the fillets with lime juice. Sprinkle with seasoned flour and grill about 5 - 7 minutes on each side or until the fresh flakes easily on both sides. Alternatively, fry the fish in a non-stick pan with a very little oil till done.

Hollandaise Sauce : Boil the vinegar, peppercorns and water in a small saucepan till reduced by one third. Strain into a double boiler (or place on a pan of hot water) and add the egg yolks. Whisk over a very low heat until the sauce begins to thicken. Divide the butter into portions and whisk it into the sauce, a portion at a time. Season and add a few drops of lemon juice.

Fish Florentine

This is a very tasty fish gratin served on a bed of spinach.

Ingredients

For the fish : 400 gm bhetki or surmai fish, cut into 4 darnes.
A little salt and pepper. 1 tbsp butter. 1 cup fish stock.
1 tsp lime juice. Pinch dried thyme.

Sauce mornay : 2 tbsp butter. 3 tbsp flour. 1½ cups milk.
½ cup fish stock. 1 egg yolk. 3 tbsp grated cheese.

You will also need : 400 gm spinach. 1½ tbsp butter.
½ tsp grated nutmeg. Salt and pepper to taste.

For the fish : Poach the fish in the above ingredient for 10 minutes or till done. Remove fish and strain stock. Keep aside.

Sauce mornay : Melt the butter in a saucepan. Saute the flour, then add the milk and fish stock (this is liquid in which the fish was cooked). Stir well and cook for 2 minutes. Add the cheese and remove from heat when melted.

Add the egg yolks, beating rapidly. Put on low heat again and stir for 1 minute. Don't let it boil or the sauce will curdle.

Spinach : Remove the stalks and roughly chop the spinach; quickly blanch in hot water for one minute. Refresh with cold water. Squeeze to get rid of moisture.

Saute spinach in butter and sprinkle salt, pepper and nutmeg. Place in a baking dish.

Squeeze the fish pieces in a dry cloth to remove water & place on top of the spinach. Pour the sauce over fish. Bake in 400°F/200°c over for 15-20 minutes until golden and bubbling.

Serves 4

Mandarin Fish

A most sophisticated example of the chinese cuisine. Try it in your kitchen; I guarantee delicious result.

Ingredients

1 large pomfret. 2 eggs. 1½ tbsp flour. Pinch salt.
Refined oil for frying.

For the gravy : 2 tbsp refined oil. 100 gm mushrooms, finely sliced. 100 gm bamboo shoots, sliced. 100 gm chicken, shredded. 2 spring onions, julienned. 150 ml chicken stock. Salt and pepper to taste. 1 tsp dark soyabean sauce. 2 tsp light soyabean sauce. Little salt. 1 tbsp cornflour.

Clean fish, but keep whole. Make two slits on both sides, on the fleshiest parts. Make a batter of the eggs, flour and salt. Coat fish with it. Heat enough oil for deep frying in a skillet and fry fish till golden, Remove.

For the gravy : Heat 2 tbsp oil left from frying the fish. Add the mushrooms, bamboo shoots, chicken and spring onion. Saute for 5 minutes. Add the stock or water, salt, pepper and both kinds of soyasauce, cook, uncovered, on high heat for another 5 minutes.

Add the cornflour mixed with a little water, stirring continuously when the gravy thickens and becomes shiny, remove from fire.

Pour over the fried fish and serve hot with fried rice or sauteed noodles.

Serves 4

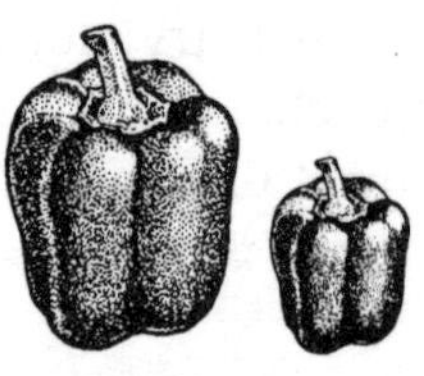

Chicken

Tomato Waldorf

Brinjals, capsicums or even large onions can be filled the same way and are good as an eatree, light meal or an accompaniment to a main course.

Ingredients

6 large, ripe red tomatoes.

For the stuffing : 2 tbsp refined oil. 1 onion finely chopped. 125 gm mushrooms, chopped. ¼ cup cashewnuts, chopped. 2½ cups chopped cooked chicken. ½ cup raisins. ¼ cup chopped parsby or fresh coriander. 2 tbsp hung curd. Salt and pepper to taste.

For the white sauce : 3 tbsp butter. 3 tbsp flour. 3 cups milk. 3 tbsp heaped grated cheese, little salt and pepper. ¼ cup heaped grated cheese for topping.

Cut the tops off the tomatoes. Spoon out the pulp, being careful not to break the shell. Place tomatoes upside down to drain.

For the stuffing : Heat the oil in a frying pan. Add the onion and fry till soft, about 5 minutes. Add the mushrooms and cashewnuts and fry for another 5 minutes until the mushrooms have wilted.

Place the chicken, raisins, parsley or coriander, and curd in a bowl. Add the fried mixture and mix well. Season with salt and pepper.

For the white sauce : Melt the butter in a saucepan. Add the flour and fry till the raw smell disappears, but do not let it to colour. Take off heat and add the milk. Stirring well so no lumps form. Cook till it thickens slightly add 3 tbsp cheese and stir till the cheese melts. Season with salt and peper.

The finale : Place the stuffed tomatoes in a greased baking dish. Pour the white sauce on the tomatoes. Sprinkle ¼ cup grated cheese on top.

Bake at 350 ° F / 160 ° C preheated oven for 15 - 20 minutes. Sprinkle parsley on top and serve hot with bread rolls.

Serves 6

Chicken Kiev

This is probably the best known of all the Russian dishes. Warn your guests what is in the middle of the golden ball or their plates - if they attack too ferociously, the butter will spurt. The fresh bread crumbs give a real soft and crisp outside to the chicken.

Ingredients

4 chicken breasts. 1 tbsp Worcestershire sauce. 1 tbsp capsico sauce, 2 tsp mustard powder. Salt and pepper to taste. ¼ cup seasoned flour. 4 eggs, beaten. 300 gm fresh bread crumbs. Refined oil for frying.

For the batter : 100 gm butter. 1 tsp grated lime rind. 4 tsp lime juice. Salt and pepper to taste. 2 tbsp chopped parsley.

Place each chicken breast between 2 sheets of dampened greaseproof paper and beat with a meat mallet or a heavy knife until quite thin. Rub with the sauces, mustard powder, salt and pepper. Keep aside for half an hour.

In a bowl, beat together the butter and lime rind. When the butter softens, add the lime juice slowly, beating all the time. Add salt, pepper and parsley and mix well in. Turn the butter out onto a sheet of non-stick paper, roll up and chill.

When the butter is firm divide into 4, placing 1 piece in the centre of each piece of chicken. Fold the chicken in rounds and secure with cocktail sticks.

Dip each piece of chicken in the seasoned flour, then in the beaten egg and roll in the fresh breadcrumbs. Chill for 15 minutes. Repeat the egg and crumbing process a second time to give a thorough coating. Chill for 1 - 2 hours. The chicken may be fried immediately, but a short time in the refrigerator helps to make the coating firm.

Heat enough oil in a karahi for deep frying and fry 1 - 2 chicken at a time until golden brown.

Take out of the oil, remove cocktail sticks, drain on absorbent paper and keep warm in the oven at 300 ° F while you fry the remaining portions.

Serve with a salad and a relish.

Serves 4

Chicken Rumaki

Hungarian Goulash is what most of us know of Hungarian cuisine. But there's lot more. Try the following simple yet delectable baked chicken.

Ingredients

1 kg chicken, cut into regular pieces. 2 tbsp butter. 2 onions, quartered and divided into segments. 2 sweet limes (mausambi) thickly sliced. Salt and pepper to taste.

For the glaze : ½ cup raisins. 1 tbsp malt vinegar. 1 tbsp honey. ¼ cup any red jam. ¼ cup sweet fruit chutney. 1 tbsp water.

Wash and thoroughly dry the chicken pieces. Brush all over with melted butter.

Grease a baking dish and arrange the onion and sweet limes at the bottom. Place the chicken pieces on top. Bake in a preheated 180 ° C / 360 ° F oven for 45 minutes or until golden brown.

Remove and spoon the glaze over the chicken. Return to oven and bake for a further 20 minutes or until cooked through.

To prepare the glaze : Place all the ingredients in a small saucepan and heat until boiling, about 2 minutes and use.

Serves 6

Maroccan Chicken Tajine

This warming dish is specially eaten in the mountains of Morocco, where it can be very cold. It takes its name from the traditional earthenware dish with a domed lid which is called tajine. You can use meat instead or omit it altogether and use chick peas.

Ingredients

1½ tbsp refined oil. 1½ tbsp butter. 1 kg. boneless chicken, cubed. Pinch turmeric, salt and pepper to taste. 1 large onion, finely chopped, 4 cloves garlic, crushed, a generous pinch of saffron. 1 tbsp ground cummin, 1½ tsp paprika or Kashmiri chilli powder. 1 tbsp brown sugar. 1 cup chicken stock. 2/3 cup raisine. 1 green chilli, chooped. 1 tbsp fresh coriander. 1 tbsp parsley.

Heat the oil and butter in a casserole and fry the chicken with turmeric, salt and pepper on high heat for 3-4 minutes, until light brown, stirring frequently.

Add the onion, garlic, green chilli and stir fry for another 3-4 minutes. Stir in paprika, cumin, brown sugar and mix well. Pour in the stock and bring to boil, adding saffron. Stir continually.

Cover casserole and place in 350 ^{0}F oven for 20 minutes. Remove from oven, add raisins. Cover and return to oven. Bake for another 20 minutes or until the chicken is very tender.

Remove and serve at once.

Serves 6

Jamaican Jerk Chicken

This is the Jamican way of spicing chicken or meat before baking. I have used chicken; meat or pork is also good cooked this way.

Ingredients

1 kg. chicken, cut into regular pieces. grated rind and juice of 1 lime. Salt to taste. 1 tsp Capsico sauce. 1 tsp dried thyme. 1/3 cup refined oil. 1 large onion, chooped fine.

Grind together : 2 cloves garlic. 2 spring onion, white part only. ½ tsp coriander seeds. 1 tsp grated ginger. 5-6 all spice. 2 cm piece cinnamon. 2 fresh red chillis. 5-6 peppercorns.

Marinate the chicken in the ground paste, rind and juice of the lime, salt, capsico sauce and dried thyme for 3 hours.

Grease a baking dish and place the chicken side by side with the marinade.

In the meantime, saute the onion in the oil till light brown. Pour over the chicken in the baking dish. Bake at 190 ^{0}C/ 380 ^{0}F oven for 30 minutes or until fully cooked.

Serve at once garnished with fresh thyme, green chillis and lime wedges.

Alternatively, instead of baking, saute the chicken in a non-stick skillet, till done.

Serve 6

Chicken Mandalay

There was a time when chicken was a special occasion dish. It was considered an expensive luxury. Over the years chicken has become easily available and simply another choice of meat. Happily, chicken can be cooked in literally hundreds of ways. The following is a Vietnamese speciality and a particularly good one.

Ingredients

1 large chicken, cut into 16 pieces. 2 tbsp chooped lemon grass. 1 tbsp curry powder. Salt and freshly ground pepper to taste. 1 tsp sugar. ½ cup refined oil, 3 sweet potatoes. Peeled and cubed. 4 cloves garlic. Finely chopped, 1 large onion, cut in wedges and divided into segments. 3 bay leaves. 2 cups water, 1 large carrot, sliced, 2 cups thick coconut milk.

Combine the curry powder, salt, pepper and sugar and rub into the chicken pieces. Marinate for one hour.

Heat the oil and fry the potatoes till lightbrown. Remove. Leave all but 2 tbsp oil in the pan and add the garlic. Stir fry till aromatic. Add the lemon grass, onion and bay leaves and stir for a couple of minutes.

Add the chicken and stir over high heat for 3-4 minutes. Add 2 cups water and carrot. Cover and bring to the boil; turn down heat and cook for 20 minutes, stirring occasionally.

Add potatoes and coconut milk. Cover and cook till the potatoes and chichen are done. There should be a thickish gravy. Serve over noodles.

Serves 4

Bhuni (Bangladesh)

An ordinary, everyday recipe. But it tastes and smells so good that I always include it in my parties.

Ingredients

1 kg chicken, cut into bite sized pieces. 100 gm curd. 4 medium potatoes. ½ cup refined or mustard oil. Salt to taste. 3/4 tsp turmeric. ½ tsp chilli powder. 1 tsp cuminseeds. 1 tbsp ghee. 1 tbsp whole garam masla. 2 bay leaves. 2 dry red chillis.

Grind together : 2 large onions, 2.5cm piece of ginger. 6 cloves of garlic. 2 green chillis.

You may use boneless chicken, cut into small pieces; in that case use 500 gm chicken only.

Beat the curd and marinate chicken in it for one hour. Peel and cut potatoes into small cubes.

Heat half the oil in a karahi. If using mustard oil, let it smoke well. Smear the potatoes with a little salt and ¼ tsp turmeric. Fry the potatoes, stirring till done. Remove, straining well.

Add the remaining oil to the karahi and temper with the cuminseeds. When they stop spluttering add the ground paste and fry, stirring till the moisture evaporates. Add the chicken and salt. Cover and cook, stirring often.

When the chicken is three fourths done add the fried potatoes. Cook, stirring well till the chicken is completely done and oil surfaces. There is no need to add any water.

In a separate pan, heat the ghee. Add the garam masala, bay leaves and dry chillis. Fry well and pour the whole thing over the chicken.

Fry for another 2 minutes, stirring well. The potatoes may get broken, but that's okay.

Serve hot with rotis and parathas goes well with rice, too.

Serves 4

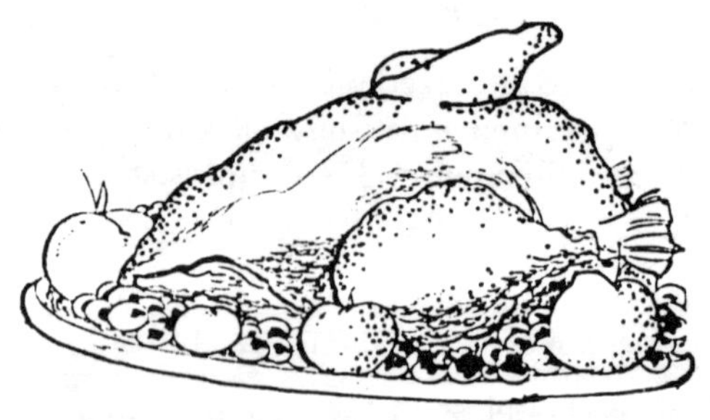

Chicken Roast

Chicken roast is immensely popular all over the world. This recipe is for oven roasted chicken with gravy.

Ingredients

1½ kg oven ready chicken. 50 gm butter. salt and pepper to taste. 2 tsp mustard powder. 1 tbsp Worcestershire sauce. 5 button mushrooms, sliced. 1 capsicum, chopped. 1 tomato, chooped. 1½ cups stock. 1½ tbsp flour.

Preheat oven to 380⁰F / 190⁰C, 10 minutes before roasting the chicken.

Thoroughly wash the chicken inside and outside with water. Drain well and dry with paper towels. Place 10 gm of butter inside the bird.

Tuck the wings and neck neatly under the bird. Truss the chicken neatly with clean string so the wings are secured to the body and the legs are held together.

Place the chicken in a roasting tin, smear all over with butter, salt, pepper and mustard. Bake chicken in the centre of the oven for 1½ - 1¾ hours, basting frequently with the pan juice.

To test whether the chicken is cooked, pierce with the tip of a small pointed knife at the thickest part of the thigh to allow juice to run out this should be clear with no trace of pink. Remove chicken and keep hot.

Carefully skin all but 2 tbsp of the fat from the roasting juice left in the bottom of the pan.

Place roasting tin on heat and add the flour. Stir till smooth. Pour in the chicken stock, capsicum, tomato. Worcestershire sauce and mushroom. Bring to the boil, stirring all the time untill the gravy thickens. Reduce heat and simmer for 5 minutes.

Pour some of the gravy over the chicken and pass the rest in a sauce boat.

Serve chicken with roasted potatoes (these can be roasted alongwith the chicken), sauteed cauliflower florets and garlic bread.

Serves 4 - 6

Chicken and Broccoli Hollandaise

Ingredients

500 gm each breasts, legs and thigh portions of chicken. 2 tsp salt. ¾ cup Hollandaise sauce. ½ cup cream, 750 gm broccoli. ¾ cup grated cheese.

For the white sauce : ¼ cup butter. 3 tbsp flour. 2 cups milk. ½ tsp grated nutmeg.

Pressure cook the chicken with enough water and salt for 7 minutes. Let the chicken cook in the liquid. Divide the broccoli into florets and cook till crisp tender. Drain.

White Sauce: Melt butter over moderate heat in a skillet. Stir the flour to make a smooth paste. This is known as 'roux'. Remove from heat and gradually add the milk. Stirring canstantly. Return pan to heat and cook for 2-3 minutes, stirring, until the sauce is thick and smooth. remove pan from heat and stir in a little salt, pepper and nutmeg.

Stir the hollandaise sauce into the warm white sauce. Beat the cream till thick and fold into it.

When the chicken is cook enough to handle, drain and slice the meat in large pieces, discarding the bones.

Arrange the broccoli in a large ovenproof dish sprinkle half the grated cheese over it. Arrange the chicken pieces on top. Pour the sauce over it sprinkle the remaining cheese.

Bake in preheated 190⁰C / 380⁰F oven for 30 minutes or until the top is golden brown. Serve immediately.

Serves 4

Ingredients

4 chicken breasts, boneless. 1 cup diced carrot, leek a celery. 1 medium onion, chopped. 3 cloves garlic, shredded. 10 pepper corns. 4 bay leaves. 2 cups grape juice. ¼ tsp salt. ½ cup seasoned flour, refined oil for frying. 2 tbsp refined wine, parsley and chopped tomato for garnishing.

For the vegetables : 2 bay leaves. 5 peppercorns. 1 cup diced carrot, leek and celery, combined. 1 medium onion, chopped. 1 tbsp butter. 1 tbsp sugar. 100 gm mushrooms, quartered. 5 pickled onion.

Marinate the boneless chicken breasts in diced vegetables, onion, garlic, pepper corns, bay leaves, grape juice and salt for 1 hour at room temperature.

Take out the chicken, coat with seasoned flour and fry in oil till golden keep aside. Add 2 cups of water to the marinade and cook for 15 minutes. Strain stock; discard vegetables.

Vegetables : Heat 2 tbsp oil in a frying pan. Add the bay leaves and peppercorns. Saute diced carrot leek celery and onion for 5 minutes. Add the strained stock and 1 cup of water. Let cook for 15 minutes.

Strain this stock over the chicken and cook over high heat till chicken is done and gravy thick. Add the red wine. Cook one minute and remove.

In the meantime, heat butter and add sugar. Let it caramelise. Add mushrooms. Toss and saute for 5 minutes. Add the pickled onions, salt and pepper. Toss and remove.

To serve : Place the chicken pieces on a serving plate. Put the gravy on them spread mushroom mixture on top.

Garnish with parsley and diced tomatoes.

Serves 4

So named because the dish uses both chicken and egg. Oyako means mother and daughter in Japanese.

Ingredients

1 chicken, cut into pieces. Salt and pepper to taste. 4 cups chicken stock. 4 onions, finely chopped. ½ cup shelled green peas. 8 button mushrooms, sliced 4 eggs. 4 tsp refined oil for frying eggs.

Pressure cook the chicken in 4 cup of water and salt for 10 minutes. Strain and reserve stock. Debone and slice chicken.

Place the stock in a saucepan. Add chicken, onion, peas, mushroom and pepper. Cook for 15 minutes.

Fry the eggs separately.

Divide soup between 4 individual soup bowls. Place a fried egg in the centre of each. Sprinkle pepper.

Serve with rice.

Serves 4

Andalusian Chicken (Spain)

This is something like a spicy stew.

Ingredients

½ cup refined oil. 1-1.2 kg chicken, cut into regular pieces. 8 button mushroom, sliced. 1 tbsp butter. 2 carrots, cut into rounds. 2 onions. 8 French beans, topped, tailed and halved. 1 cup shelled peas. salt and pepper to taste. 3 tsp curry pd. 4 cups chicken stock. ¾ cup rice.

Bouquet garni : Tie in a string 1 stalk of parsley. 1 bay leaf. 1 stick celery.

Heat the oil in a skillet. Add the chicken and brown all over. You will have to do it in batches. Drain.

Saute the mushrooms in butter for 2 minutes

In a large saucepan, combine the carrots, onions, French beans, peas, bouquet garni, salt, pepper, curry powder and hot stock or water. Add the chicken, cover and cook for 20 minutes over a medium heat.

Wash and add the rice and mushrooms, cook for another 20 minutes. Serve hot.

Serves 6

Thai Chicken Red Curry

The food of Thailand is unique among the cuisines of South East Asia. It has the quality and consistency of Chinese food and the spicness of Mexican. Whether red hot or comparatively bland, balancing flavours lie at the heart of good Thai cooking.

Ingredients

1 kg chicken. 8 tbsp refined oil. 2 lime leaves. 4 green chillis, chopped. 2 tbsp heaped red curry paste. 4 cup thick coconut milk. 2 tbsp fish sauce. 2 tsp sugar. 2 tbsp chopped basil. Salt and pepper to taste.

Red Curry Paste : 15 dry red chillis. 1 bunch spring onion. 2 tbsp grated ginger. 4 tbsp chopped garlic. 2 lime leaves. 4 stalks lemon grass (white part only). 1 tbsp roasted coriander and cuminseeds, each. 20 peppercorns. 1 tbsp coriander leaves. 3 tbsp refined oil. Blend all the ingredients in the processor.

Parboil the chicken. Drain well and saute in 4 tbsp oil till light brown on both sides. Remove.

Add the rest of the oil and fry lime leaves and green chillis. When aromatic, and the red curry paste and fry for 2 minutes, sprinkling a little water. If necessary.

Add the coconut milk, fish sauce, sugar, salt and pepper. Stir in the chicken when it comes to a boil. Let cook till the chicken is done and gravy thick. Add the basil and remove.

Serve with fried rice or plain noodles.

Serves 6

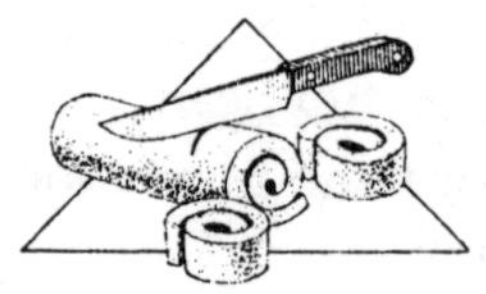

Chicken And Broccoli Gougere

This is an unusual but easy recipe; followed by a fruit and coffee it is ideal for a light lunch.

Ingredients

For the Choux Pastry : 1 cup of water. 60 gm butter or magarine. 1 cup flour. 2 eggs.

For the filling : 600 gm chicken pieces. 1 large head broccoli. 1 cup milk. 3 tbsp cornflour. 100 gm grate cheese. ½ tsp salt. 1 tsp freshly ground pepper.

Chonx Pastry : Put the water and butter or margarine into a saucepan and bring to the boil. Remove from heat, add the flour all at once, beat vigorously.

Return to low heat and stir until the mixture is smooth and in one lump, then cool slightly. Add the eggs, one at a time, beating well after each addition.

Butter the sides of a circular 25 cm ovenproof dish. Surround it with spoonfuls of the chonx pastry, leaving a hollow in the centre.

Pour in the prepared chicken and broccoli filling and bake in preheated 200^0 C / 400^0 F oven for 30 minutes.

Filling : Choose breasts, legs and thigh portions of the chicken; in other words, the fleshly parts. Cook in lightly salted water till done. Remove flesh from bones and cut into strips.

Cut the broccoli into small florets. Cook in boiling salted water for 5 - 7 minutes. Drain.

Heat the milk in a saucepan. Mix the cornflour with a little milk and add, stirring constantly. Lower heat, gradually mix in the cheese. Stirring continuously, allowing cheese to melt between each addition. Cook till thick season with salt and pepper, then add chicken and broccoli. Mix well.

These can be baked in individual pans also.

Serves 4

Chicken Khowsuey

Ingredients

1.5 kg chicken. 1.2 lt. stock or water. 300 gm noodles. 4 large onions. ½ tsp turmeric, ½ tsp garlic paste. 1 tsp ginger paste. 1 tsp green chilli paste, salt to taste. ½ cup refined oil. 1 tbsp gram flour.

Grate the coconut and blend with 1 cup of hot water. Strain. Extract 2 more cups of coconut milk likewise. Keep all the extractions together.

Cook the noodles and keep hot. Slice 2 onions and crush the other two. Rub chicken with turmeric and pressure cook with the water for 7 - 8 minutes, with salt to taste. Remove the bones and shred the flesh. Crack the bones and add to the stock which continues to simmer.

Rub the chicken with the crushed onion, ginger, garlic and green chilli paste.

Heat the oil in a non-stick skillet. Add the onion and stir fry for 2 minutes. Add the chicken and saute for another couple of minutes. Pour the strained stock and simmer.

Make a paste of the gram flour and little stock. Add to the chicken, stirring constantly. Cook for 15 minutes.

Finally add the coconut milk. Continue cooking for 5 minutes more. Check for seasonings and serve over hot noodles.

This is traditionally served with the following accompaniments - 4 chopped hardboiled egged, chopped spring onion, lime wedges, deep fried chopped garlic.

Serves 4

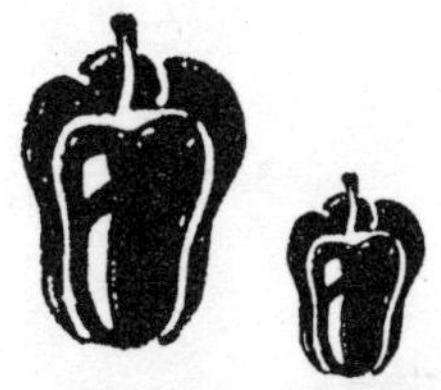

Fried Chicken In Lemon Sauce (Hong Kong)

For all the lovers of Chinese food, a trip to Hong Kong is a must. It offers an astounding variety of flavour of all the regions of China.

Ingredients

500 gm boneless Chicken, cut into pieces. 2 eggs. 2 tsp white wine or vinegar. 2 tsp soyabean sauce. 5 tbsp cornflour, refined oil for deep frying, fresh coriander for garnishing.

For the sauce : 1½ tbsp lime juice. 2 tsp sugar. 1 cup chicken stock. Salt and white pepper to taste. 1 tbsp cornflour.

Beat the eggs. Combine the egg with the wine or vinegar, soya sauce and cornflour. Mix the chicken with it and marinate for 30 minutes. Add the cornflour and deep fry the chicken till done. Cook over medium low flame, turning occassionally. Remove and drain thoroughly.

Arrange chicken on a serving plate. Pour the lemon sauce and garnish with fresh coriander springs.

Sauce : Mix the lime juice, sugar and stock in a small saucepan and slowly bring to boil. Reduce heat and simmer for 5 minutes, stirring until the sugar has dissolved. Mix the cornflour with a little water; add to the sauce and stir for another minute or until the sauce is thick and glossy.

Serves 4

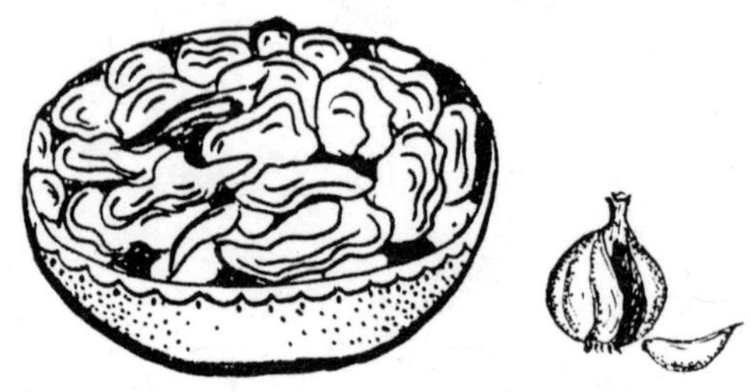

Meat

Crisp Crust Mutton Flar

Try this unusual idea of cold crisp pastry and mutton.

Ingredients

Crust : 1 cup crushed potato chips. 2 cubes of cheese. grated. 50 gm butter.

Filling : 350 gm boneless mutton. 2 tsp ginger paste. 1 tbsp freshly ground pepper, 1 tbsp gelatine. ½ cup cream, 3 egg whites. Salt to taste.

Crust : Mix the chips and cheese together. Add melted butter and mix thoroughly. There's no need to add salt. Since all the ingredients are salty.

Firmly pat the bottom and sides of a circular baking dish. Bake in an oven preheated to 350^0F / 180^0C for 10 minutes. Cool and chill till needed.

Filling : Cut the mutton in very small pieces. Combine the ginger paste and pepper with mutton keep aside for half an hour. Add salt and pressure cook with ½ cup of water for 15 minutes. Evaporate excess water, if any, let cool.

Soak the gelatine in 1/3 cup of water for 15 minutes. Dissolve over very low heat.

Mix the cream and mutton. Add dissolved gelatine. Beat egg whites till stiff and fold into the meat.

Pour into the baked shell. Chill till needed. Serve cut in wedges.

Orange Steak

In Australia, steaks and chops are eaten for breakfast too, and the fruit flavour is highly enjoyed. It packs a change from the ordinary. Prime quality beef steaks is used for this. I've substituted mutton. But feel free to use steak.

Ingredients

4 thick pasandas, ¼ cup raw papaya juice. 4 tbsp butter. Juice of 2 oranges and 1 lime.

For the stuffing : ¼ cup butter, grated ring of 1 orange and 1 lime. 1/3 cup diced or soaked prunes or dates. 1 cup fresh breadcrumbs. Salt and pepper to taste. 1 tbsp orange juice.

Slit the meat halfway across to make a pocket. Rub the raw papaya juice inside and out and marinate the meat in it for 4 hours or preferably overnight. Squeeze and drain excess water. Pat dry with clean kitchen towel.

To make the stuffing : Soften the butter slightly and blend with all the remaining. Press together firmly; divide into 4 portions and insert one portion in each pocket of the pasanda.

Tie with thread or secure with wooden picks to prevent stuffing from falling out.

Blend 4 tbsp butter with orange and lime juice. Brush the meat pasandas generously with the butter and grill in a hot oven for 2-3 minutes. Turn over and baste with the fruit juice and grill, rotating and basting till done. Alternatively, fry the meat in butter, using a non-stick pan.

Serve with mashed potatoes, mixed with a little grated nutmeg. Arrange meat on top of the potatoes, Garnish with orange slices and parsley.

Serves 4

Enchiladas

Mexican culinary skills is perhaps the closest to their Indian counterparts; only the latter is richer in spices. For the tortilla - see the recipe of burritos.

Ingredients

For the filling : 1 capsicum. 1 onion. 100 gm carrot. 100 gm French beans. 6 cloves garlic. 2 green chillis. 1 tbsp butter. 1 tbsp refined oill. 1 cup cooked minced meat.

For the tomato sauce: ½ kg. ripe, red tomatoes, 2 tbsp refined oil. 1 large onion, finely chopped. 5 cloves garlic, chopped. 2 tbsp sugar. 2 tsp chilli powder. Salt to taste. 1 tbsp vineger.

To Assemble : 1 cup thick white sauce. ½ cup grated cheese. Few capsicum rings.

For the tortialla - cook according to the recipe of the burritos.

To make the stuffing : Finely chop all the vegetables, garlic and green chillis.

Heat the butter and oil in a skillet and sante the onion, garlic, green chilli, capsicum till soft. Add the mince, carrot, beans and salt. Fry for 3 - 4 minutes till everything is well mixed. Remove.

To make the tomato sauce : Blanch, peel, deseed and puree the tomatoes in a mixer. Strain.

Heat the oil in a frying pan; sante the onion and garlic till light brown. Add the tomato puree and rest of the ingredients. Cook medium heat till the sauce is thick, stirring continually.

To assemble : Grease a baking dish. Dip each tortilla in the sauce. Put filling in the centre of each tortilla and roll neatly. Arrange the rolls in the baking dish, seam side down. Pour left over sauce over it.

Cover with the white sauce, sprinkle cheese and lay the capsicum rings decoratively. Bake at 220⁰C preheated oven for half an hour. The white sauce may be omitted, if desired. Vegetarians - omit the mince and used cooked rajma puree instead.

Serves 8

Lasagne Verdi

This world wide favourite Italian dish is a hassle to make, but to compensate for this the preparation and assembling can be done in advance, making it a wonderful one dish meal.

Ingredients

12 sheets lasagne. 75 gm grated cooking cheese.

Bolognaise Sauce : 3 tbsp butter or refined oil or a combination of the two. 1 onion, chopped. 2 cloves garlic, chopped. 2 stalks celery, chopped. 450 gm mince. 250 gm tomatoes, chopped. 2 tbsp tomato puree. 300 ml chicken stock pinch grated nutmeg. 100 gm mushroom, sliced. Salt and pepper to taste generous pinch of dried thyme.

Bechamel Sauce : 600 ml milk. 1 bay leaf. 6 peppercorns a large pinch of grated nutmeg. 1 small onion, quartered.2½ tbsp butter. 2½ tbsp flour, pinch of salt. 1 tsp freshly ground pepper.

Cook lasagne sheets in boiling salted water with 1 tbsp oil added. Drain in a colander and rinse with cold water. Lay on absorbent paper to dry.

Meanwhile prepare the Bolognaise sauce. Heat the butter or oil in a saucepan. Add onion, garlic and celery and saute until the vegetables start to soften. Add the mince and salt, stirring, until browned all over, and free of all lumps. Add tomatoes, stock, puree, mushroom, salt, pepper and nutmeg. Cover and simmer till done. A pressure cooker may be used. Dry away excess liquid, in that case.

Bechamel Sauce : Place the milk, bay leaf, peppercorns, nutmeg and onion in a pan. Bring slowly to boil. Remove and let cool.

Melt the butter in a frying pan and stir in the flour. Cook one minute. Stir in the strained infused milk, stirring so no lumps form. Bring to the boil and cook stirring for 1-2 minutes till a little thick.

To assemble : Lightly grease a deep baking dish. Line with 4 cooked lasagne sheets and spread half the bolognaise sauce followed by 1/3 bechamel sauce. Continue this way ending up with a layer of bechamel sauce sprinkle the cheese on top.

Bake in preheated 200^0 C / 400^0 F oven for 40 - 45 minutes until browned and bubbling.

Serves 4 -6.

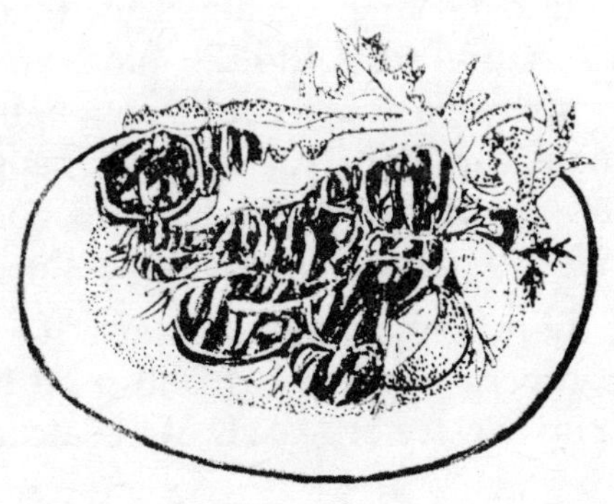

Moussaka

Thousand of travellers to Greece and the Aegean return with appetities whetted for greek food. A favourite is delicately flavoured moussaka - a casserole of brinjal, mince, tomato sauce, cheese and herbs. Its a complete meal, inexpensive and perfect for informal entertaining. The yogurt topping gives it a new dimension.

Ingredients

450 gm brinjals, refined oil for frying. 1 large onion. 4 cloves garlic. 650 gm minced meat. 4 large tomatoes. 1 large capsicum. 1 tsp Kashmiri chilli powder or paprika. salt and freshly ground pepper to taste. 2 tbsp tomato ketchup, pinch of dried oregano or ½ tsp crushed ajwain. 150 ml stock.

Topping : 2 tbsp flour. ½ tsp baking powder. 3 eggs. 150 ml fresh curd. 2 cubes cheese, grated.

Slice the brinjals and place in a single layer on a plate. Sprinkle with salt and leave for 30 minutes. The salt will draw out excess juices which can taste bitter when cooked.

Chop the onion, and garlic. Blanch the tomatoes, peel, remove seeds and chop. Core, deseed and chop the capsicum.

Heat 2 tbsp oil in a frying pan and saute onion and garlic for 5 minutes or until soft. Add the mince and continue to fry, breaking up the meat as it cooks, until lightly browned. Add the tomato, capsicum, paprika, salt, pepper, ketchup, oregano or ajwain and stock. Bring to the boil. Cover and simmer for 25 - 30 minutes. It should be thick fairly dry.

Meanwhile, thoroughly drain and rinse the brinjals; pat dry with absorbent paper. Heat 2 tbsp oil in a large on stick frying pan and fry brinjal slices in batches till golden on both sides. Do this quickly on high heat. You will have to add more oil. Remove fried brinjals onto an absorbent paper.

Grease an ovenproof dish and layer the brinjals and mince mixture alternately beginning and ending with a layer of brinjals.

For the topping : Sift the flour, baking powder and a pinch of salt. Gradually beat in the eggs and then the curd. Pour this evently oven the moussaka and sprinkle the grated cheese.

Bake in preheated 350^{0}F / 180^0 C oven for 40 minutes, untill the topping is well risin, crisp and golden brown.

Serve with a salad and crusty bread.

Moussaka can be heated a day ahead, refrigerated and reheated just in time of serving.

For a vegetarian version use paneer or soya granules in place of mince. You may use a topping of white sauce in place of the curd mixture.

Serves 6.

Mexicalli Pancake

Golden corn pancakes filled with spicy mince and topped with tomato sauce, make a tempting meal for any occasion.

This recipe has three stages :

1. Tortilla : 1 cup cornmeal (Makki ka atta) ¼ cup flour. 1 tsp salt.

2. Mexican Sauce : 1 large onion. 1 large capsicum. ¼ cup refined oil. 750 gm blanched tomatoes. ½ cup tomato ketchup. 8 cloves garlic. 1 tsp salt. 1 tsp sugar. 1 tsp mustard powder. 1 tsp chilli powder.1/6 cup vinegar. 1 tsp lightly roasted and crushed cuminseeds.

3. Fillings : ½ cup cooked minced meat. ½ cup finely chopped onion. ½ cup grated cheese. ½ cup shredded lettuce or cabbage. Salt and chilli powder to taste. ½ tsp cumin powder.

1. Tortilla : Mix the cornmeal, flour and salt. Add enough hot water to form a soft dough. Divide the dough in 12 parts. Roll each part to the size of a puri. Quickly bake on a hot tawa. Cover with a napkin and keep aside.

2. Mexican Sauce : Finely chop the onion and capsicum. Heat the oil, saute onion and capsicum till soft. Blend the blanched tomatoes and garlic in the mixer. Add to the sauteed onions alongwith the rest of the ingredients except cuminseeds cook till the sauce thickens. Remove from heat and add the cumin.

3. Filling : Mix all the ingredients together and use.

The finale : Preheat oven to 450^{0}F / 225^{0}C. Dip each tortilla in mexican sauce. Place a little filling on top. Roll tightly. Place in a greased 25 cm baking dish; cover with the remaining sauce and grated cheese. Bake 20 minutes.

For a vegetarian version use paneer or cooked rajma.

Serves 6.

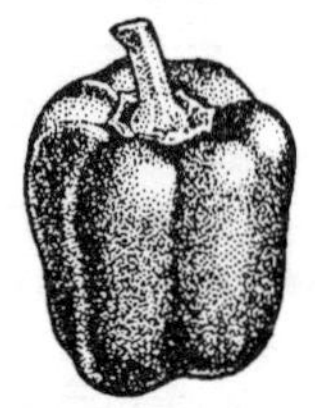

Rezala (Bangladesh)

When I first tasted Rezala, what struck are most was how different from most mughlai dishes it was in its colour and by the complete absence of chilli powder. Having a curd based gravy, it has a pale colour, slightly off white, pinkish quite unlike the rich reddish brown of most north Indian and mughlai curries.

Ingredients

1 kg meat. 250 gm curd. 1½ tbsp ginger paste. 1 tbsp garlic paste. salt to taste. 1 tbsp freshly ground pepper. 1 tsp garam masala powder. 250 gm onions, thinly sliced. ½ It. full cream milk. 2 tbsp cashewnut paste. 2 tbsp ghee. 4 bay leaves. 4 dry red chillis. 1 tbsp cuminseeds. 200 ml refined oil.

The meat should preferably be from the breast portion and with a little fat. Have it cut into medium pieces. Beat the curd and add to the ginger garlic paste, salt, pepper, garam masala powder, onion and refined oil. Mix well and add the meat. The marinade must coat the meat well. Refrigerate for 6 hours.

In the meantime, boil the milk till reduced by half, add to it the cashew paste keep aside.

Heat the ghee in a heavy bottomed degchi. Temper with the dry red chillis, bay leaves and cuminseeds. When the seeds pop up, add the meat and its marinade.

Fry over a medium heat, stirring continually to begin with. This takes a lot of time. No water is to be added. The meat will release a lot of its own water.

Stir more frequently later. By the time the water dries up and the oil surfaces, the meat should be done. Add the kheer mix and stir for another 5 minutes.

Remove and serve hot with naan or paratha.

Serves 6.

Add the scrambled eggs, green chillis and salt to the mince and mix.

Heat enough oil in a heavy tawa. Moister your hands and take a large lime sized mince in your hand. Add straight to the tawa and shape into a rough tikia on the tawa itself. The kabab won't be smooth and will be rather uneven in shape. Fry on both sides till golden.

These are very soft and tender Kababs, liable to break; so handle very carefully.

Makes 25-30

Bobotie

A much loved dish from South Africa, flavoured with spices and apricot chutney, topped with a savourty custard and baked until set and golden.

Ingredients

3 tbsp apricot chutney or 50 gm dry apricots. 2 large slices bread. 1½ cups milk. 2 onions. 2 cloves garlic. 3 tbsp refined oil. 4 bay leaves. 5 cm cinnamon. 3 green cardamoms. 1 tbsp grated ginger. 1 tsp coriander powder. 1 tsp cumin powder. 500 gm minced meat. Salt and pepper to taste. 1 tbsp sugar. 50 gm raisins. 1 apple, peeled and chopped. 1 tbsp vinegar. 300 ml stock or water. 50 gm flour. 2 eggs.

If using dry apricots. soak them overnight. Discard the stones and chop. Discard the crusts of the bread and soak in a little water; mash till smooth. Finely chop the onion and garlic.

Fry the onion and garlic in oil until soft, but not browned. Add bay leaves, cinnamon, cardamom, ginger, cumin and coriander and cook for 2-3 minutes, stirring continously. Add the mince and bread and break up with a spoon. Stir in salt and pepper and cook till lightly browned.

Stir in the raisins, apricots chutney or chopped apricots, apple, sugar, vinegar and stock. Cook till the mince is done. The resulting mixture should be very thick. If there is a lot of water left, boil very fast to reduce. Place the mince in a greased ovenproff dish. Sift the flour with salt and pepper. Put the eggs and milk in a bowl and beat with a fork. Stir in the flour.

Make a smooth batter. Pour over the mince mixture. Bake in preheated 200 ^{0}C / 400 ^{0}F oven for 20 - 30 minutes or until golden brown and set.

Serve at once with plain cooked rice or a simple pulao.

Scotch Broth (Scotland)

Traditionally pearl barley is used for scotch broth, for convenience I have used rolled oats. This can be served as an one dish meal.

Ingredients

1 small carrot. 1 medium potato. ½ kg meat. 1 cup shelled peas. 1 cup cauliflower florets. ½ cup diced green beans. ½ cup rolled oats. Salt and pepper to taste a rasher of bacon. 1 cup fried bread crontons, lime wedges to serve with.

Peel and cube the carrot and potato. Cut meat in small pieces. Pressure cook meat in 5 cups of lightly salted water for 20 minutes. Drain stock and reserve. Remove meat from the bones and put back into the stock.

Put stock back on the heat. When it comes to a boil, add the vegetables salt, pepper and oats. When the vegetables and cereal are tender, remove.

Fry bacon till very crisp. Remove rind and cruble. Sprinkle into the soup.

Serve in individual bowls with croutons of bread on top; pass around a plate of lime wedges.

Serves 4.

Variation : Instead of oats, a handful of rice may be added.

Aab Gosht (Pakistan)

Ingredients

8 mutton chaaps, each about 100 gm. 2 tsp ginger paste. 1 tsp garlic paste. 1 tsp green chilli paste. ½ tsp garam masala pd. 1 tsp rose petal, ground. Salt to taste. 150 gm onion. 100 gm refined oil plus oil for frying onions. 150 gm curd. 3 tbsp khus khus paste. pinch of saffron. 3 drops sweet itar. 1 tsp roasted and powdered cuminseeds and coriander leaves for garnishing.

Wash and dry the mutton chaaps. Mix together the ginger, garlic, green chilli paste, garam masala powder, rose petal paste and salt. Rub this well into the meat chaaps and marinate for one hour.

Slice the onions evenly and thinly. Heat enough oil for frying in a degchi. Add the onion slices and fry over a medium heat. Stirring continously, till an even golden. Take out over a piece of paper and let extra oil drain.

When cool enough to handle, blend in mixer with curd.

Heat 100 ml oil in the degchi. Take the meat from the marinade and fry lightly. Remove.

In the same oil, add the curd mixture and khus khus paste and marinade. Fry stirring continously for 2 minutes. Add mutton and fry for another 5 minutes. Add saffron and itar.

Cover and seal the degchi with atta dough. No water is to be added. Cook on a very low heat for half an hour. Or till done. You may keep a tawa underneath the degchi for the last 10 minutes.

Serve hot garnished with cuminseeds and coriander leaves.

Serves 4

Matka Pasanda (Pakistan)

Ideally, this should be made in an earthen matka. But a degchi does just as well.

Ingredients

1 kg 250 gm pasanda, each weighing 50 gm. 4 tbsp green papaya paste. 1½ tbsp garlic paste. 75 ml refined oil. 200 gm onion, ground. 1 tsp chilli pd. 150 gm curd. salt to taste. 150 gm birishta, ground 1 tsp garam masala powder. 10 small potatoes, fresh coriander for garnishing.

To make birishta : Take 4 large onions and evenly slice them. Fry in enough oil over medium heat till golden. Stir continously or the onions will burn. Remove onto a piece of paper so extra oil can drain. When cool and crisp, grind to a paste.

Pasandas are flat, boneless pieces of meat. Its a special cut of meat; each piece has to be beaten with a meat mallet till thin. The meat seller will do it for you. Alternatively take large boneless pieces of meat and beat with a meat mallet to thin it down somewhat. Mix the raw papaya paste, cashewnut paste and ginger garlic paste together and rub the pasandas with it using your hands. Marinate for half an hour.

Heat the oil in a degchi. Add the ground onions and stir fry till light brown. Add chilli and fry 2 minutes more. Take off heat and add curd, stiring well. Put on heat again. This ensures that the curd does not curdle.

Add the marinated pasandas and fry stirring well. When the oil separates, add salt and birishta paste. Put on a slow heat and fry stirring a few times. Remove when done. There should be a thick gray. Sprinkle garam masala pd. and remove.

Garnish with potato fingers and coriander leaves.

Serves 6 -8

Shepherd's Pie (U.K.)

If there's one dish thats very British, its the pie. A pie can be sweet or savoury and may have just a bottom crust of pastry or a crust enclosing the filling. The 'Shepherd's Pie' has no pastry on top but there is layer of potatoes to cover it.

Ingredients

Topping : 900 gm potatoes, salt to taste. 300 ml milk. 1½ tbsp butter. 2 eggs. 4 tbsp grated cheese. ¼ tsp freshly grated nutmeg.

For the mince : 1½ tbsp groundnut oil. 700 gm minced meat. 2 large onions, finely chopped. 150 ml stock. 1 bay leaf. Salt and freshly ground pepper to taste. 1 tbsp Worcestershire sauce. 1 tsp made mustard.

Topping : Peel and quarter the potatoes. Cook in salted water, till done. Drain. Mash. Melt the butter in the mixie over a gentle heat. Add the potatoes and mash till smooth. Remove. Separate the eggs. Add the yolks, cheese, nutmeg and salt. Mix well. Whisk the egg whites stiffly and fold into potatoes.

Mince : Heat the oil over high heat. Add the mince, breaking lumps, if any. Add the stock, bay leaf, salt and pepper. Cover and cook on low heat till the mince is done and dry. Add the Worcestershire sauce and mustard grease a baking dish. Spread the mince mixture in the pan evenly. Spoon or pipe the potato mixture decoratively on the mince to cover it completely.

Bake in an oven preheated to 400 ⁰F / 200 ⁰C for 30 minutes.

Serves 6

Burritos

A myth about Mexican food is that it is mouth burning, full of chillis and heavy. In fact, contrary to belief, onions, coriander and tomatoes form the main ingredients of Mexican cuisine not chillis. However green chillis (Jalapeno) are generously used in most dishes but only for the "tang" and not to burn down the tastebuds.

Ingredients

For the tortillas : 1 cup cornmeal (makki ka atta). ¼ cup flour, 1 tsp salt.

For the filling : 1/3 cup refined oil. 4 cloves garlic, minced. 1 large onion. finely chopped. 1 tsp paprika. 1 bay leaf. 1 tsp dry mixed herbs (thyme, basil, oregano). 2 large tomatoes, chopped, 4 green chillis, chopped. 250 gm minced meat. 100 gm kidney beans. cooked and ground to a rough paste. Salt to taste.

For the tortilla : Mix the cornmeal, flour and salt. Pour in enough hot water to form a dough. Divide the dough in 12 parts. Roll each part to the size of a puri. Keep covered.

For the filling : Heat the oil in a skillet. Add the garlic and onion and saute till pink. Add the paprika, bay leaf and herbs. Try till aromatic.

Add the tomatoes and green chillis. Saute till the tomatoes are soft. Now add the mince and stir fry till no longer pick and free of all lumps.

Add the cooked kidney bean paste and mix well. Add enough water and cook till done and dry.

The finale : Take one tortilla. Place one cheese slice on it. Top with one part of filling. Cover with another tortilla and seal with flour paste. Shallow fry on a tawa. Serve hot.

Serves 4

Minted Mutton Chops

Served with bread rolls, this constituted a whole meal; most refreshing during summer.

Ingredients

1 kg meat chops. 2 cups of water. 1 stock cube. 2 green chillis. Salt and pepper to taste 1 tsp heaped cornflour. 2 tbsp finely chopped mint. 1 lime.

Pressure cook the meat with the water. Stock cube, green chillis, salt and pepper for 8 minutes. Strain. Keep cooked chops refrigerated.

Bring the stock to a boil. Mix the cornflour with a little cold stock and add to it alongwith salt, pepper and mint. Cook on low heat. Stirring till slightly thickened. Add the lime juice and remove. Cool and refrigerate.

Pour the minted sauce over the chops and serve with finger chips. Garnish with mint springs.

Serves 6

Cold Cut

Indians are not used to eating cold food, though our country being a tropical one, has at least 6 months of intense heat in a year. Do try this cold cut during summer; you'll love it.

Ingredients

1 kg leg of mutton. 1 tbsp sugar. 1 tbsp ginger paste. 1 tbsp garlic paste. 1 tbsp Kashmiri chilli powder. 1 tbsp malt vinegar. 1 tbsp lime juice, salt to taste. ¼ cup refined oil. ¼ cup butter.

Keep the leg of mutton whole. Ask your butcher to debone it & discard the inner tenden also. Wash the mutton & dry thoroughly. Prick all over with a fork. Roll and bind with a string at 3-4 places. This is to ensure that the meat does not get out of shape while cooking.

Mix the sugar, ginger garlic paste, chilli powder, vinegar, lime juice and salt together; you may also add pepper to taste. Rub onto the meat.

Heat the oil and butter together in a large skillet, preferably a non-stick one. Add the meat and cook over high heat. Do not stir. The hot oil with seal the meat and keep the juices in. Turn the meat over only when you can do it easily. Brown the other side, too.

Add 2 cups stock or water and cook for 15 minutes in a pressure cooker. Open cooker only when it cools. Take out the meat. Drain well & cover with aluminium foil. Refrigerate for 4 -6 hours or longer.

Measure the stock left in the cooker. It should be 2 cups. If necessary, make up with water. Let it come to a boil, add 1 tbsp flour mixed with ¼ cup cold stock; stir continually. Let cook till thick. Add salt and pepper. Keep hot.

Take out the meat, cut in slices and serve with the hot sauce and sauteed boiled vegetables. Serve bread and butter on the side.

Serves 6

Vegetables

Baba Ghanouj

Very good starter, dip or a side dish.

Ingredients

1 large brinjal. 1 tbsp lime juice. 1 tbsp chopped green chilli or to taste. 1 tbsp crushed garlic. ½ cup chopped dill. 4 tsp heaped tahina. 1 small onion, grated and squeezed dry. Salt to taste.

Roast the eggplant. Peel and blend with the garlic. Add lime juice, green chilli, dill, tahina, squeezed onion and salt. Mix well.

Serve with pita bread wedges or baby naans.

Tahina : Tahina or Tehina in all its various forms is a great Middle Eastern favourite, it is served as an accompaniment to most cold and some hot dishes. The main ingredient is sesame seeds. It keeps indefinitely.

1 cup toasted sesame seeds. 3 cloves garlic. ¾ - 1 cup water. 1 tsp cuminseeds. Juice of 2 limes salt and pepper to taste.

Grind the toasted sesame seeds, cuminseeds and garlic together. Place them in a blender and gradually add the water. If prefered you may strain the mixture.

To this add the lime juice, salt and pepper. It is almost as thick as mayonnaise.

Serves 6

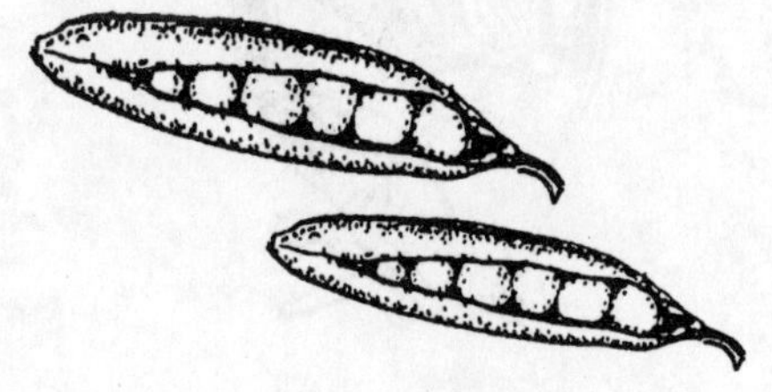

Ratatouille

There are a number of different versions of this wonderful vegetable dish. It is most versatile. It makes an excellent filling for pancakes and pies. or, make a whole meal served with fluffy rice and a crisp salad.

Ingredients

2 tbsp olive oil or refined oil. 2 large onions, chopped. 1 tsp chopped garlic. 2 red capsicums, seeded and chopped. 450 gm courgettes or bottle ground, sliced. 400 gm tomatoes, blanched, peeled and chopped, salt and freshly ground pepper to taste, a handful of chopped parsley.

Heat the oil in a skillet and saute the onion. when soft and transparent, add the garlic, capsicums and courgettes and stir for another 5 minutes.

Add the tomatoes, salt and pepper, cook gently for 15 minutes until the vegetables are tender. If the vegetables have released a lot of water, dry away excess liquid over high heat.

Serve garnished with lots of parsley.

Serves 4

Ghivecin

An unusual Rumanian vegetable stew with a fascinating combination of vegetables and fruits Ghivecin exists in countless interesting variations throughout the Balkans. Middle East and Caucasus. Its particularly good with fish, chicken and meat.

Ingredients

1 large brinjal. 3 carrots, scraped and sliced. 4 potatoes, peeled and sliced. 4 onions, sliced, 3 celery stalks, sliced. 6 tomatoes, blanched and peeled. 1 large capsicum, seeded and sliced. 1 small cauliflower, separated into flowerettes.100 gm French beans, topped, tailed and cut into 2.5 cm lengths. 1 cup shelled peas. Salt to taste. 2 tsp freshly ground pepper. 4 tbsp chopped parsley or dill. 2 cloves garlic, finely chopped. 2 tbsp refined oil. 100 gm grapes. 50 ml tomato puree. 1 cup chicken stock.

Dice and sprinkle the brinjal with salt. Keep for half an hour, then squeeze to rid of water. Wash and squeeze dry again.

Arrange the vegetables and grapes in layers in a large ovenproof casserole. Sprinkle each layer with a little salt and pepper, parsley or dill.

In a small saucepan, heat the tomato puree and stock. Pour the liquid over vegetables. Sprinkle the oil.

Cover and bake at 180°C / 350 °F preheated oven for 1 - 1½ hours or until the vegetables are done. Serve at once.

Serves 6

Chlodnik

Here is an unusual and highly satisfactory Polish soup, perfect for a summer meal. I often serve it as a desert after a heavy menu.

Ingredients

2 apples. 2 pears. 250 gm plums. 2 oranges. 1 tbsp orange rind, 4 tbsp sugar or to taste. 1 tsp ground cinnamon. ¼ tsp powdered cardamom. 450 ml apple juice. 1 cup green grapes. 1 cup black grapes. 150 gm yogurt cream chantilly. 4 tbsp almond slivers.

For the yogurt cream chantilly : 150 ml cream. 3 tbsp icing sugar or to taste. 1 tsp vanilla essence. 150 ml hung curd.

Peel and quarter the apples and pear; quarter and deseed the plums. Divide the orange into membrane free segments.

Combine the apples, pears, plums, orange sections, orange rind, sugar, cinnamon, cardamom and apple juice in a stainless steel saucepan. Cover and simmer for half an hour or till the fruits are soft.

Serve hot or chilled garnished with grapes, yogurt creme chantilly and almonds.

To make the yogurt creme chantilly : Beat the cream over ice till it begins to stiffen. Add the icing sugar and vanilla and continue to beat until stiff. Fold in the curd gently but thoroughly. This can be refrigerated for several hours.

You may add any fruit puree of your choice to the creme chantilly for a different dessert altogether.

Serves 4

Potato and Mushroom Zharkoye

Russian cookery, do not, as a rule use Soya sauce as a flavouring ingredient. But I find its inclusion does wonders for the taste. Hence I've taken the liberty.

Ingredients

700 gm potatoes. 1 tbsp refined oil. 250 gm button mushrooms, coarsely chopped. 1 large finely chopped onion. 1 clove garlic, minced. 3 tbsp light soya sauce. ½ cup water. 2 tbsp curd. Salt and pepper to taste.

Cook the potatoes until done; but do not overcook. Drain well; peel and mash smoothly.

Heat oil in a Karahi. Add the onion and garlic and fry till soft and translucent. Add the mushrooms. Salt and pepper. Cook, uncovered, stirring continually till the mushrooms release their water, Add soya sauce and cook over low heat till the sauce becomes thick and a rich brown.

Finally add the curd and mix well.

You can serve it in two ways. Either pour the gravy over the mashed potatoes and serve. or, put the potatoes in the pan after curd and mix lightly and remove. Serve hot.

Serves 6

Potato Latke

When the festival of Hanukkah (commenorating the victory of Judas Maccabeus over the Seleucids of the 2nd Century B.C.) comes round, Israelis and Jews celebrate by making a sort of potato pancake called Latke which is deep fried in oil, Latkes, when correctly made are crisp, light and dry - never oily.

Ingredients

2 large potatoes. 1 large onion. 1 large egg. beaten. 2 tbsp cornmeal or whole wheat flour. Refined oil as needed for frying. Salt and freshly ground pepper.

Wash and roughly grate the potatoes and onion. Do not wash there after. Put them in a muslin cloth and squeeze out as much of the starchy liquid as possible. Transfer potato mixture to a bowl.

Stir in the cornmeal or wheat flour, salt and pepper. Combine gently to mix.

Heat enough oil in a skillet for deep frying. Take spoonfuls of the potato mixture and drop in the hot oil.

Flatten slightly with the back of a spoon. Fry for a few minutes until the latkes are golden brown underneath, turn over and continue frying till golden.

Drain on absorbent paper and serve hot with a chutney or relish. To give an Indian flavour add finely chopped green chillis and coriander leaves.

Serves 4

Variation : Instead of deep frying, drop spoonfuls in a lightly oiled non-stick tawa, Press each down with back of a spatula to make thin pancakes. This makes it easier to cook. Fry both sides to golden.

Frijoles Refritos

Many Mexican recipes call for refried beans - which is actually cooked rajma. Keep a pot of it in the refrigerator as a standby.

Ingredients

¾ cup kidney beans. 1½ tbsp refined oil. 2/3 cup chopped onion. 2 cloves garlic minced. 2 tsp cumin powder. ¼ cup diced capsicum. Salt and freshly ground pepper to taste. 2 tbsp chopped coriander leaves.

Soak the beans overnight and cook till done. Drain and reserve stock.

Heat the oil in a skillet and saute the onions and garlic. When the onions soften, add the capsicum and cumin and saute for another 5 minutes until the onions begin to brown.

Add the beans and salt; continue stirring for 2 minutes. Remove the skillet from the heat; using a potato masher, thoroughly mash the beans while adding as much of the stock as necessary to reach a soft, spreadable consistency. Add pepper to taste and chopped coriander leaves.

This is wonderful as a topping for crisp tortillas, a filling for quesadillas or a side dish for a Mexican meal.

Serves 4

Cheese and Tomato Charlotte

If you have any stale or hard cheese sitting in your refrigerator, this is a fine way of using it.

Ingredients

4 large slices bread. 4 tbsp refined oil. 2 cups tomato puree. 175 gm grated cheese. 1 large onion, grated. 1 tbsp finely chopped parsley. Salt and pepper to taste.

For the sauce : 300 ml stock. ½ cup tomato puree. 1 tbsp cornflour. 1 tbsp chopped spring onion. 1 tbsp chopped parsley. 1 tsp made mustard. 1 tsp Worcestershire sauce. Salt to taste.

Cut the bread into fingers. Heat the oil in a frying pan and fry the bread until brown.

Mix the tomato puree with cheese. onion, parsley, salt and pepper. Put half the bread in a baking dish. Top with the cheese and tomato mixture, then the rest of the fried bread. Bake for 20 - 25 minutes at 190^0 C / 380^0 F oven.

Meanwhile make the sauce : Combine the stock and tomato puree. Blend the cornflour. Pour into a saucepan and stir over medium heat until thickened. Add the onion, parsley, mustard, Worcestershire sauce and salt. Cook till thickened and well blended.

Serve with the sauce.

Serves 4

Potato Pizza

This 'Pizza' made of mashed potatoes and with a choice of three fillings, is a speciality of Pugalia in Northern Italy.

Ingredients

For the base : 300 gm potatoes. 100 gm flour 1 tsp baking powder. ½ tsp salt. 50 gm butter.

Topping No. 1 : 200 gm onions, sliced. 1 capsicum, chopped, 100 gm cheese, thinly sliced. 1 tbsp refined oil. 2 tbsp tomato ketchup. 100 gm button mushrooms, sliced, ½ tsp oregano, 2 tsp vinegar. Salt and pepper to taste.

Topping No. 2 : 200 gm onions, finely chopped. 2 cups shelled prawns. 2½ tbsp flour. 300 ml milk. 2 tbsp chopped parsley. Salt and pepper to taste. 2 cubes cheese, grated.

Topping No. 3 : 6 large tomatoes. 250 gm sausages. 1 small onion, chopped. 1 tsp basil. 2 tbsp tomato ketchup. Salt and pepper to taste. 1 cube cheese, grated.

To make the base : Boil, peel and mash potatoes smoothly. If the potato is hot, stir in the butter, then add the flour (sifted with baking powder) and salt. If the potato is cold, rub the butter into the flour before stirring into the potatoes. Khead lightly then place dough on an greased baking sheet and press into 25 cm round.

Topping No. 1 : Heat the oil. Fry the onion and capsicum gently for 2 - 3 minutes. Spread the ketchup over the potato base. Stir mushrooms, oregano, vinegar. Salt and pepper into the onion, then spread over base and arrange the cheese slices all over. Bake at 400⁰ F / 200⁰ C preheated oven for 40 minutes or until the base is firm and the cheese a rich golden.

Topping No. 2 : Cook the prawns and drain. Fry the onions gently until they start to soften. Stir in the flour, then milk and bring to the boil, stirring all the time.

Remove pan from heat and stir in the prawns, parsley, salt and pepper.

Carefully spoon the sauce over the pizza base. Sprinkle the cheese over top and bake.

Topping No. 3 : Blanch, peel, seed and chop the tomatoes. Cook the sausages and halve them lengthwise.

Mix the tomatoes, onions, basil, ketchup salt and pepper together and spread over the base. They lay the halved sausages over the top like the spokes of a wheel. Sprinkle cheese in between the sausages and bake.

Serve hot, cut in wedges.

Serves 6

Bread and Cheese Pudding

This savoury pudding is Switzerland's contribution to your kitchen. Serve it once. Your family will certainly ask for an encore.

Ingredients

8 thick slices bread. Butter as needed. 175 gm grated cooking cheese. 300 ml chicken or vegetable stock. 2 eggs, beaten, 75 ml cream. Salt and pepper to taste.

Generously butter the bread on one side only. place half the bread, buttered the side up in a greased baking dish and sprinkle cheese on top. Cover with the remaining slices, buttered side down.

Combine the stock, eggs and cream. Season with salt and pepper. Pour over the bread and let soak for 30 minutes.

While the bread is soaking, press it down several times to make sure the top layer is moistured by the egg mix.

Bake in an oven preheated to 180⁰C / 350⁰F for 45 minutes or until golden and slightly crisp.

Serve hot.

Serve 4

Barbecue Tofu Chilli

400 gm tofu or paneer, cubed. 2 tbsp refined oil. 2 tbsp chopped garlic. 4 green chillis. finely chopped. 1 capsicum, julienned. 1 onion, cut into wedges and divided into petals.

For the barbecue sauce : 1 tbsp oyster sauce. 1 tbsp green chilli paste. 1 tbsp soyabean sauce. 1 tbsp vinegar. 1 tbsp tomato ketchup. 1 tbsp jaggery or brown sugar. Salt to taste. pinch of monosodium glutamate. ½ tsp chilli sauce. 1 tsp grated ginger. ¼ tsp chilli powder. 1 cup chicken stock or water.

Heat the oil in a non-stick skillet. Add the garlic and saute for 1 minute. Add the green chillis, capsicum and onion and stir fry for 2 minutes.

Combine all the ingredients for the sauce and pour into the pan. Let it come to the boil. Add the tofu or paneer and cook, till most of the moisture evaporates.

If you want it gravied, add 1 tsp cornflour and cook till thick.

Serve garnished with spring onions.

Serve 6

Mixed Fruit Curry

This incredible curry from Sri Lanka is my all time favourite. Please note that all the fruits must be just ripe and firm and not unduly soft, or they will break during cooking.

Ingredients

1 banana, ½ honeydew melon (Kharbuja), 100 gm green grapes, 100 gm black grapes, 1 orange, divided into membrane free segments, 1 red apple. 1 cup cubed pineapple, 75 gm coconut cream. 2 tbsp curry paste. 2 tbsp curd. 1 tbsp sugar. 1 cup cream. Salt to taste. 1 tbsp refined oil.

For the curry paste : 1 tsp coriander seeds. 1 tsp cuminseeds. 1 tsp fennel seeds. 1 tbsp rice. 2 tbsp desiccated coconut. 1 dry red chilli, 2 cm piece of cinnamon. 4 cloves. 4 green cardamoms 2 tsp grated ginger. 1 tbsp vinegar.

To make the curry paste : Roast the coriander cumin, fennel seeds, rice and desiccated coconut on a dry pan, stirring continously until they become fragrant and darker in colour. Remove and let cool.

Place the roasted spices into the blender container. Add the chilli, cinnamon cloves, cardamoms, ginger and vinegar. Blend to a paste, adding a little water to assist movement of blades. Remove.

To make creamed coconut : Grate 2 large coconuts and take out the milk using 4 cups of hot milk, using one cup of water at a time. Keep all the extractions together in the refrigerator. In the morning you'll find the cream solidified on top. Take out and use. Discard the liquid.

Peel and slice the banana. Peel and cube the melon. Core and slice the apple but leave the skin on to add colour. Heat the oil in a saucepan and add the curry paste. Stir over a low heat till the oil separates. Add the coconut cream, when it melts, remove from heat and add the curd, well beaten, stirring continously.

Add salt, and sugar and let cook for 5 minutes. Add the fruits; stir with a light hand for 3 - 4 minutes or untill fruits are warm.

Remove onto a serving dish and serve at once with rice.

Serves 2 - 4

Cashewnut Curry from Sri Lanka

Sri Lanka was an important centre for the spice trade in the 15th and 16th Century. No wonder Sri Lankan cuisine is marked by the use of spices.

The following curry powder has quite different characteristics from Indian curry powder. It can be used for poultry, meat or vegetable curries. It will keep for six months stored in an airtight tin.

Ingredients

225 gm cashewnuts. 1 medium onion. 2 green chillis. 1½ tsp curry powder. ½ tsp turmeric. 250 ml coconut milk. ¼ tsp chilli powder. 1 tsp salt. ½ tsp fenigreek seeds. 1 spring of curry leaves. 2 tbsp refined oil. Salt to taste.

For the curry powder : 6 tbsp coriander seeds. 3 tbsp cuminseeds. 1 tbsp fennel seeds. 5 cm piece of cinnamon. 8 cloves. 8 green cardamoms. 6 dried curry leaves. 1 tbsp rice. ¼ tsp turmeric. 1 tsp chilli powder.

Soak the cashewnuts for a couple of hours. Chop the onion and green chillis.

Remove the cashewnuts from water and place in a saucepan alongwith the green chillis, 1 tsp curry powder, turmeric, coconut milk, chilli powder. Salt, fenigreek seeds and curry leaves. Bring to the boil and simmer for 5 minutes.

Heat the oil in a frying pan and toss in the onion for a couple of minutes. Add the cashewnuts mixture and cook for a further 3 - 4 minutes, then sprinkle the remaining curry powder and remove.

For the curry powder : Dry roast all the ingredients except the turmeric and chilli powder. Remove from heat and when still hot add the turmeric and chilli powder. grind to a powder. Store in an airtight container.

Serves 4 -6

Minestone

An one dish meal - full of the goodness of peas and beans. The macaroni provides the necessary carbohydrate.

Ingredients

250 gm white beans. 2 tbsp refined oil. 1 large onion, chopped. 2 cloves garlic, minced. 8 cups stock or water. 1 large carrot, diced, 2 sticks celery, sliced. ½ small cabbage, shredded. 2 large tomatoes, blanched, peeled and chopped. 1 cup sliced beans. 1 cup shelled peas. 1 tsp dried oregano. Salt and freshly ground pepper. 1 tsp sugar. 1 cup elbow macaroni, or any other small shaped pasta. ½ cup chopped parsley. 2 cups freshly grated cheese.

Soak the beans overnight and cook till done.

Heat the oil in a large saucepan. Saute the onion and garlic till soft. Add all the ingredients except macaroni, parsley and cheese. Cover and cook gently for one hour.

Stir now and then. After half an hour of cooking add the macaroni and parsley.

Stir to mix everything well and serve in individual soup bowls sprinkled with a little cheese. Serve the remaining cheese separately.

Serves 8

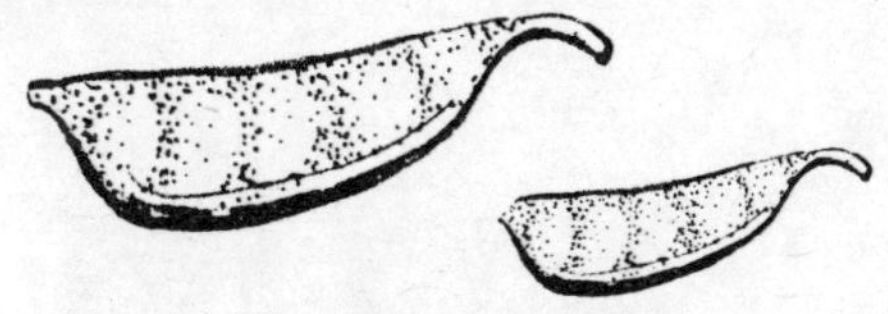

Jacket Potatoes

Popular all over the continent, jacket baked potatoes are cheap, filling and delicious served with a selection of savourty toppings.

Ingredients

4 large potatoes. 1 - 2 tbsp refined oil. 1 tsp salt.

Scrub the potatoes thoroughly and pat dry. Rub a little oil over the skins and smear with salt. Place in a baking tray and make sure they don't touch. You may thread the potatoes lenghtways on to metal skewers. The metal conducts the heat quickly to the centre of the potato, so reducing the cooking time.

Bake in preheated 200^{0} C / 400^{0} F oven for 1 - 1¼ hours or until soft when pierced with a fine needle.

When cool enough to handle split the potatoes in halves and scoop out the inner portion with the help of a spoon leaving a 1 cm wall and taking care not to break the skins.

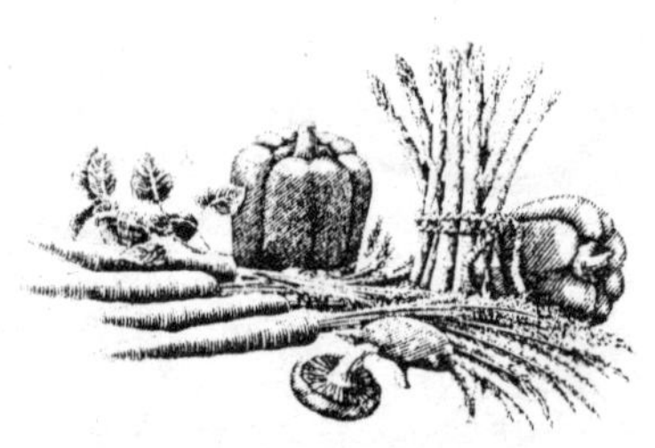

Souffle Potatoes

Ingredients

3 tbsp butter. 3 tbsp cream. 2 egg yolks. 3 cubes cheese, grated. Salt and pepper to taste. 2 egg whites.

Mash the scooped out potatoes with all the ingredients except the egg whites whisk the egg whites till stiff and lightly fold into the potato mix. Carefully spoon into the potato skin and sprinkle the grated cheese.

Bake in preheated 190^0 C / 380^0 F oven for 15 minutes.

Piquant Prawns

Mix 150 ml mayonnaise with 2 tbsp tomato ketchup and 3 drops of capsico sauce. Stir in 175 gm of cooked prawns and 1 tbsp chopped parsley. Mix in the potato pulp and proceed as per the previous recipe.

Chutney Chicken

Ingredients

1 small onion, finely chopped. 1½ tbsp butter. ½ tsp curry pd, or to taste. 3 tbsp tomato ketchup. 2 tbsp mango chutney or any other chutney of your choice. Salt and pepper to taste. 150 ml mayonnaise. 225 gm cooked chicken nuggets.

Saute onion in butter until soft. Add the curry powder. Stir 1 minute. Add the ketchup, chutney, salt and pepper. Stir 2 minutes. Cool; stir in mayonnaise and chicken. Mix with mashed potato and fill the potato skins. Bake as usual.

Egg and Hollaindaise Sauce Topping : 100 gm butter. 2 egg yolks. 1 tsp lime juice, generous pinch of salt and pepper. 4 eggs, peached.

The butter should be at room temperature. Whisk the egg yolks with 1 tbsp butter in a small pan. Whisk in the lime juice and cook over a very low heat or in a double boiler adding salt and pepper. Continue whisking until the mixture has thickened slightly, then gradually whisk in the remaining butter, a little at a time, whisking until the sauce is very thick.

Place one poached egg inside each potato half and pour over the sauce. This does not need further baking.

Besides these, any leftover curry, chicken tikka, chilli chicken, chilli con carne etc. can be used to fill the potatoes. So let your imagination work. There are really no limit to what you can fill baked potatoes with.

With a soup and a salad this makes a complete satisfying meal. Mustard, chutney ketchup and mayonnaise make tasty accompaniments.

Serves 4

Cocido (Portugal)

Equally popular in Spain. Very good for those on a diet. It completely eschews the use of fat or oil.

Ingredients

½ cup white chick peas. 250 gm tomatoes. 500 gm fatless meat or 1 chicken. 1 tsp grated ginger. 3 bay leaves. salt and pepper to taste. 1 small cabbage, cut into wedges. 3 carrots, sliced. 100 gm French beans, diced. 3 tsp cornflour.

Soak the chick peas overnight. Blanch, peel and chop tomatoes.

Pressure cook the chick peas, meat, ginger, bay leaves, salt and pepper with 3 cups of water for 20 mins.

Open cooker add cabbage carrots. French beans and tomatoes. Let cook till the vegetables are tender.

Mix cornflour with little water and add to the soup. Cook 5 minutes more till slightly thickened. Taste and adjust seasonings. Use freshly ground pepper for best result.

Serve the meat and vegetables in a soup plate covered with the soup. Serve with well seasoned rice.

Serves 6

Revythia

A filling stew from greece made with chick pea and vegetables will warm the family even on the coldest days and is practically a meal in itself.

Ingredients

1 tbsp grated ginger. 4 cloves. 10 peppercorns. 1 bay leaf. 5 cups stock. 2 cups cooked chick peas. 1 medium potato, diced. 1 medium carrot diced. 1 stalk celery, chopped. 1 red yellow and green capsicum each, deseeded and cubed. 1 cup chopped spinach. salt and pepper to taste, juice of one lime. 1 tsp paprika powder. 1 tsp roasted and powdered cuminseeds, finely chopped mint for garnishing.

Tie the ginger, cloves, peppercorns and bay leaf in a muslin. This is called a 'bouquet garni'. Boil the stock in a saucepan, add the spice bundle, potato and carrot. Cook for 5 minutes. Add the chick peas. Cover and cook for 5 minutes more.

Add the celery, salt, capsicum, spinach and paprika and cumin powder. Cover and cook till done. Remove some of the chick peas and puree in the blender. Return the pureed chick peas to the boiling stew; cook for a few minutes, stirring continually for a few minutes. Check the seasonings.

Serve immediately garnished with mint.

Serves 4 - 6

Gnocchi with Tomato Sauce

Gnocchis are Italian dumplings; they are also made with gour or potatoes.

Ingredients

For the gnocchi : 750 ml milk. 1 tsp salt, pinch grated nutmeg, pinch pepper powder. 110 gm semolina. 1 egg. 120 gm grated cheese. 3 tbsp melted butter.

For the Italian sauce : 2 tbsp butter. 2 tbsp refined oil. 2 large onions, finely chopped. 2 tbsp chopped parsley. 750 gm blanched tomatoes. 10 cloves of garlic. ½ cup tomato ketchup. 1 bay leaf. salt, pepper and red chilli powder to taste. 1 level tsp freshly crushed ajwain.

For the gnocchi : Lightly grease a 23 cm square baking dish. Combine milk, salt, nutmeg and pepper in a saucepan and bring to the boil. Reduce heat and gradually stir in the semolina. Stir for about 10 minutes or until the mixture is thick. Remove from heat. Let cool for 2 minutes; stir in the beaten egg and 80 gm (1 cup) of the cheese.

Spread the mixture into the prepared tin. Refrigerate for one hour. Turn gnocchi out of pan and cut into 4 cm rounds. Place the rounds slightly overlapping on the tray. Brush with butter, sprinkle remaining cheese. Bake in preheated 180⁰ C / 360⁰ F oven for 15 minutes or until light brown.

Served topped with tomato sauce. Garnish with more cheese, if desired.

Gnocchis can be served with barbecued meat or chicken to make a complete and satisfying meal.

For the tomato sauce : Heat the butter and oil together in the skillet. Fry the onions and parsley till soft. Blend the blanched tomatoes and garlic in the processor. Add to the fried onions alongwith all other ingredients except ajwain.

Cook, stirring till the sauce is thick. Remove from the heat. Add ajwain. Mix and serve.

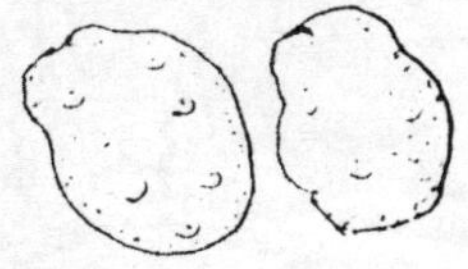

Italian Skellet Dinner

This is a vegetarian version. You may add chicken, sausage or minced meat, for a non - vegetarian variation.

Ingredients

3 cups cooked shell pasta. ½ cup grated cooking cheese.
For the sauce : 5 tbsp butter. 3 medium onion, sliced.
2 tsp chopped garlic. 2 cups quartered and boiled mushrooms.
3 cups milk. ¼ cup cream. Salt and pepper to taste. 2 tbsp flour.

Heat the butter in a large skillet. Add the onion and garlic and saute till soft and transparent. Add the mushroom and flour and cook for another 3 - 4 minutes.

Add the milk gradually, mixing well to make sure there are no lumps. Bring to boil. Add the cream, salt and pepper. Stir to mix and remove. Keep covered.

Just before serving, reheat the sauce, adding a little milk, if required and toss the pasta in it.

Serve hot garnished with cheese.

Serves 4

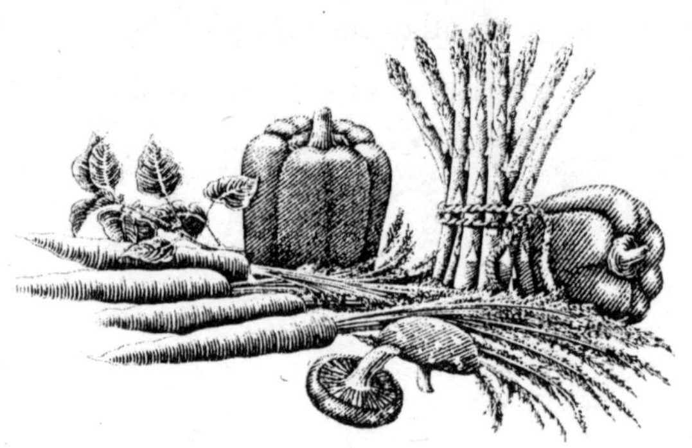

Snacks

Pizza Marguerita

The sinful cheesy slice of pizza decorated with unlimited toppings has won the hearts of food lovers in every corner of the globe.

Ingredients

For the base : 2/3 cup water. 2 tbsp fresh yeast (10 gm). 1 tsp sugar. 2 cups flour. 1 tsp salt .1 tsp oil, preferably olive oil.

For the tomato sauce : 9 large, ripe, red tomatoes. 2 tbsp refined oil. 2 bay leaves. 6 peppercorns. 1 tsp finely chopped garlic. 1 small onion, chopped. 4 tsp sugar. ½ tsp dried oregano.

For the topping : 10-12 fresh basil leaves, roughly chopped. 1 capsicum, cut into rings. 4 large sausages, cooked and sliced. 1 small onion, cut into rounds. 1 cup grated Mozzarella cheese. 2 tbsp oil, preferably olive oil.

To make the base : Heat the water to lukewarm, sprinkle the yeast, sugar, a little flour and cover for 10 minutes, by which time it will start to froth.

Sift the flour into a bowl. Sprinkle the salt by the sides. Make a well in the centre and pour in the yeast mixture. Knead into a soft dough.

The dough will be very soft and sticky to begin with; but as you go on kneading it will become pliable. Add the olive oil and knead again.

Grease a bowl lightly and place the dough in it covered with an oiled greaseproof paper. Keep in a warm and drought free place, till double in bulk, almost an hour-less in summer.

Press the dough lightly to release the accumulated air. The dough should be very soft. Divide into 2 equal parts. Roll each portion with the help of a little dry flour to a circle of

25 cm. (10 inch) in diameter and ¼ inch thick.

To prepare the tomato sauce : Blanch, peel, deseed and chop the tomatoes. Heat the oil in saucepan, add the bay leaves and peppercorns. Saute for 30 seconds. Add the garlic and onion and fry till pink.

Add the tomatoes and stir continuously for 10 minutes. Put in the salt, sugar and oregano, simmer for 20 minutes or till quite thick.

The finale : Divide the topping ingredients in two portions. Place one pizza base on a greased tray, spread half the tomato sauce on it. sprinkle on it one portion of the basil leaves. Place the onion, capsicum and sausage slices. Cover with half the cheese and drizzle half the oil all over.

Bake at 200^0 C/400^0 F preheated over for 20 minutes or till the base is evenly golden. cut into wedges and serve.

Do likewise with the remaining base.

Variation : This is the basic recipe for pizza. Use your own topping like chicken, prawns in place of sausages or omit these totally for a vegetarian version. Olives go very well as toppings.

Makes 2 pizzas

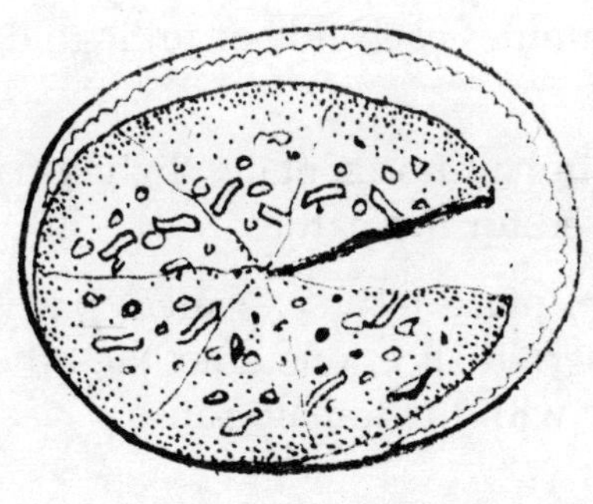

Hamburgers

Teenagers love them with a passion. And in America its a national weakness. A simple bread roll becomes a feast when layered with fillings. I give two variations.
The first one uses minced mutton, but chicken mince, ham, cheese or even vegetable fillings can be used. Serve with cole slaw, mashed potatoes and tomato sauce to make a full meal.

Ingredients

500 gm lean minced mutton. 1 small onion. finely chopped. 1 tbsp thick tomato puree. 2 tsp Worcestershire sauce. 2 tbsp fresh coriander. Salt and pepper to taste. 6 tbsp grated cheese. 4 burger rolls. 4 lettuce leaves.4 slices tomato. 4 rings onions. 4 slices gherkin.

Combine the mince, onion, tomato puree, Worcestershire sauce, fresh coriander, salt, pepper and 2 tbsp cheese in a bowl. Mix with hands till well combined. Divide into 4 portions.

Place 1 tbsp of grated cheese in the centre of each mince portion. Smoothen mince around the cheese to enclose it. Shape into a round patty.

Heat a non-stick frying pan. Brush lightly with oil. Cook patties 8-10 minutes each side or until golden and cooked through.

Cut the rolls in half horizontally, lightly fry the cut sides on the pan used for the patties.

On each base, place lettuce, a meat patty. one tomato, onion and gherkin slice, one after the other. Cover with the top. Serve with the tomato sause.

Tomato sauce : 4 large,ripe, red tomatoes. ¼ cup refined oil. 1 large onion, finely chopped. ½ cup malt vinegar. 1tsp chopped garlic. 1 tsp grated ginger. Salt and freshly ground pepper to taste. 1 tbsp sugar . 1 tsp crushed chilli flakes. Blanch, peel, deseed and chop the tomatoes. Heat the oil, add the garlic and onion and fry till pink. Add the remaining ingredients and cook over a moderate heat, stirring often till thick.

Keeps well refrigerated for at least a fortnight.

Ribon Sandwich

This is an American style loaf sandwich so popular among the young and old alike. A knife and fork are used to eat these.

Ingredients

900 gm unsliced loaf of bread.

Prawn butter : 100 gm cooked prawns.½ tsp lime juice a little mustard a little paprika. 50 gm butter.

The butter used throughout should be at room temperature. Blend all the ingredients together.

Ham Butter : 60 gm minced ham or chicken a little mustard. 50 gm creamed butter.

Mix all the ingredients together. Those who don't eat ham, used cooked minced chicken.

Egg Butter : 2 chopped hardboiled eggs. 1 tbsp grated cheese pinch chilli powder. 50 gm creamed butter.

Mix all the ingredients together.

Green Butter : 1/3 cup grated and drained cucumber. 1 tbsp chopped parsely or fresh coriander. 1 tbsp choppped sweet pickles. 50 gm creamed butter.

Squeeze the cucumber gently to drain all moisture. Mix all the ingredients together.

Remove all the crusts of the loaf. A warm and sharp knife facilitates the process. Cut the loaf into 5 horizonal slices, spread each slice with one of the butter, save one slice. Place the slices together. Top with the remaining slice. Press well so each slice adheres to the other.

Cover the top and sides of the loaf sandwich with softened cream cheese or hung curd mixed with mayonnaise and 1 tbsp powdered sugar. Use an icing bag to decorate the top as liked so that it looks like a cake chill and cut into ½ inch thick slices.

Serves 6-8.

Opera Sandwich

'Ooperavoileipa' or Opera Sandwich is a Tinnish Version of the hamburger. Its a slice of toasted french bread topped with a mutton patty, glazed with lemon sauce and then topped with a fried egg.

Ingredients

750 gm lean minced meat. 2 tbsp finely chopped onion. ½ tsp salt. ½ tsp grated lime rind 1 egg. 2 tbsp refined oil. 2 tbsp vinegar. ½ tsp ground ginger. 3 tbsp firmly packed brown sugar. 1 bay leaf. 6 thin slices of lime. 2 stock cubes. ½ cup of water. You will also need: 6 thick slices French bread, buttered on both sides. 2 tbsp butter. 6 eggs.

In a bowl, combine the minced meat onion, salt, lime rind and egg. Mix lightly and shape into 6 thick patties.

In a non-stick frying pan, heat the oil over medium high heat; add the meat patties and brown well on both sides - about 5 minutes on each side. Remove patties and set aside; discard any fat in pan. To the pan add the vinegar, ginger, brown sugar, bay leaf, lime slices, stock cube and water.

Mix cream cheese with chopped walnuts. Top with crambled eggs and a few cooked prawns.

Buttered rolls filled with tuna or prawn or chicken mixed with sweet mango chutney.

Buttered brown bread covered with shredded lettuce, topped with chicken and clotted with chilli sauce.

Polynesian Salad Open Sandwich : 3 cups cooked chicken, shredded. 1 hardboiled egg, diced. 2 sticks celery, finely chopped. 1 apple peeled, cored and diced. ½ cup raisins. Salt and freshly gound pepper to taste. 1 cup curry mayonnaise, ½ cup chopped pineapple. ½ cup sliced bananas. 1 loaf cheese bread. chopped parsley for garnishing.

Combine the chicken, egg, celery, apple, papaya, walnuts and raisins. Season lightly with salt and pepper. Add the mayonnaise and mix well. Refrigerate for an hour.

When ready to serve peel and slice the bananas; toss in lime juice and add to the chicken mix. Slice the loaf in 12 thick slices and warm them in the oven. Place the open buns on individual serving plates; divide the salad among them and sprinkle with parsley.

Serves 6

Sweet Chocolate Sandwich

Ingredients

1 recipe chocolate butter. 1 large banana. 1 cup crumbled cottage cheese. ¼ cup green grapes. ¼ cup black grapes. 3 sweet buns. chocolate sauce as needed.

Halve the buns. Spread with the chocolate butter.

Top with the cottage cheese. Then divide the banana and grapes over them. Drizzle with chocolate sauce and serve.

Serves 6

Hummus

A complete food in itself, hummus provides protein, fibre and energy together with a rich olive oil flavour. With a curd dip, bread and salad it can make a complete meal or a good starter. Hummus tastes best if kept for one or two days covered and chilled.

Ingredients

150 gm chick peas. 2 tbsp tahini. 2 cloves garlic, minced. Juice of 1 lime or to taste. 4 tbsp olive oil. Salt and pepper to taste. Paprika to garnish.

Soak the chick peas overnight. Pressure cook in fresh water for 30 minutes. Drain. Reserve stock.

Blend the chick peas, garlic, juice of 1 lime and olive oil.

Shahi Stuffed Mutton Kabab (Pakistan)

Everybody loves a platten of succulent kababs. 'Kabab' originates from a Turkish word denoting a spicy morsel of meat roasted on a skewer. It has come a long way from being just a bit of salted and barbecued meat. Now, the kabab is made to suit every taste and palate.

Ingredients

700 gm minced meat. 150 gm gram dal. 1 large onion. 1 tbsp grated ginger. 6 cloves garlic. 1 tbsp poppy seeds. 1 tsp cuminseeds. 1 tsp chilli powder. 1 tsp garam masala powder. 1 tsp pepper powder. 2 eggs, juice of 1 lime or 2 tsp amchur. salt to taste, refined oil for frying.

For the stuffing : 250 gm fish - bhetki, rohu or surmai. 1 large onion. 1 cm ginger. 2 cloves garlic. 2 green chillis. 1 tbsp refined oil. ¼ tsp garam masala powder salt to taste. ½ tsp sugar. Pinch turmeric.

Pressure cook the meat, gram dal, onion, ginger, garlic, poppy seeds, cuminseeds and salt with one cup of water for 10 minutes. Dry excess liquid, if any. The mince should have no moisture.

Grind the mince alongwith the chilli, garam masala and pepper. It should be a very tight dry dough like consistency. Mix the eggs, lime juice or amchur. Divide into 20 - 25 portions.

For the Stuffing : Steam fish till done. Remove the bones grind the onion, ginger, garlic and green chillis together.

Heat the oil in a karahi and fry the ground paste till the oil surfaces. Add the fish and remaining ingredients. Fry well for 3 - 4 minutes; remove. Divide the stuffing into 20 - 25 parts.

Take one part of the mince mixture and stuff with one portion of the filling. Roll into a ball and press slightly to give a kabab shape.

Heat enough oil in a karahi, deep fry 5 - 6 kababs at a time till golden.

Serve with chutney and salad.

Makes 20 - 25

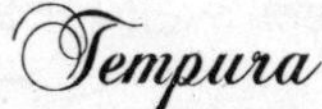

Tempura originates in Japan where it is often served with pink pickled ginger for a contrasting sharp flavour.

Ingredients

3 slices of brinjal. 1 medium potato. 6 thin florets of cauliflower and broccoli each. 4 baby corns.4 green chillis. 6 tender cabbage leaves. 6 spinach leaves. 6 thick onion rings, 1 tbsp light soyabean sauce. 2 tsp sugar. 1 tbsp lime juice. 1 cup cornflour. 1 egg separated. ¼ cup of water. Salt and pepper to taste refined oil for deep frying.

Use all or any of the vegetables. The brinjals should be cutin 1 cm thick rounds. Halve each round to form semi circular pieces. Cut the potato in ½ cm thick slices and cut again to half moon shapes. Blanch the potatoes, broccoli and cauliflower in boiling water for 3 - 4 minutes. Drain.

Combine the soya sauce, sugar and lime juice. Marinate the vegetables in it for ½ an hour.

Beat the egg yolks and water and add to it the cornflour, salt and pepper. Separately beat the egg whites until soft peaks form. Fold into the egg yolk mixture.

Heat enough oil in a karahi for deep frying. Dip the vegetables, one at a time; let extra batter flow. There should be just a thin coating of the batter adhering to the vegetables. Fry in batches over medium heat for 1 - 2 minutes, depending on the vegetables (hard vegetables will take more time), each side until a light golden. Drain on paper towels. Serve immediately.

For the ginger pickles - slice ginger thinly. Put in a dry, clean glass jar. Top with lime juice and sal t. Shake well and keep in the suen. Soon it will turn pink. Green chillis may also be added. Keeps well for a long time.

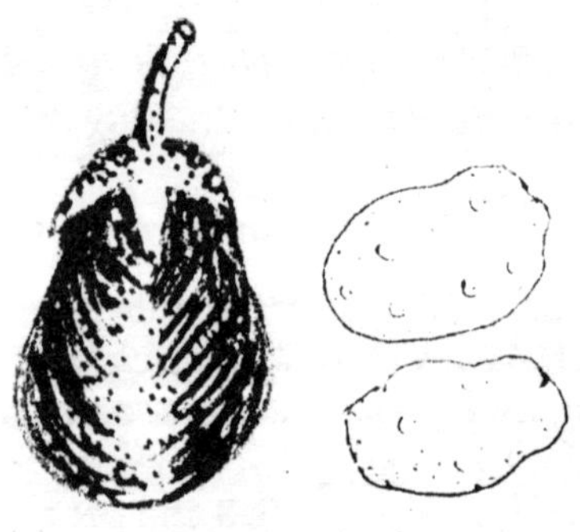

Felafel

Felafel, a snack from the middle Eastern countries is high protein and low cholestrol. Its excellent meat substitute.

Ingredients

¾ cup black eyed beans. ¾ cup chick peas. 1 large potato, boiled and mashed. 1 large onion, chopped. 2 cloves garlic. 2 tsp cumin powder. ½ tsp cinnamon powder. 1 tsp chilli powder. 2 green chillis, finely chopped. ¼ cup coriander leaves. Salt and pepper to taste.

Yogurt Sauce : 1 medium cucumber. ¾ cup hung curd. ½ cup orange juice. ½ tsp roasted and powered cumin. 1 tbsp chopped coriander leaves. 1 tsp sugar. Salt and pepper to taste.

Soak the beans and chick peas for at least 15 hours. Drain well.

Process the beans, chick peas, onion and garlic until finely minced. Mix the mashed potato well. Stir in the spices, green chilli, coriander leaves, salt and pepper.

Roll 2 level tbsp of the mixture into balls and flatten slightly. Stand for half an hour.

Heat enough oil in a karahi for deep frying, till smoling. Remove from heat, add a few balls at a time. Stir, turn once and put on medium heat once more.

Fry turning a few times till well brown. Do not fry over a high heat. The insides should cook well, too. Remove when done on absorbent papers.

Yogurt sauce. Peel and dice cucumber very small. Beat hung curd and add orange juice, salt, pepper, cumin powder, coriander leaves and sugar. Add cucumber and mix well. Use chilled.

The felafel are very good on their own, but you may even serve them in pita pochets. Spoon some of the yogurt sauce inside the pockets, fill with lettuce, bits of tomato, top with a felafel.

Kidney beans, soya beans, white beans can be used the same way. If you want you can parboil the beans and use.

Makes 15 - 20

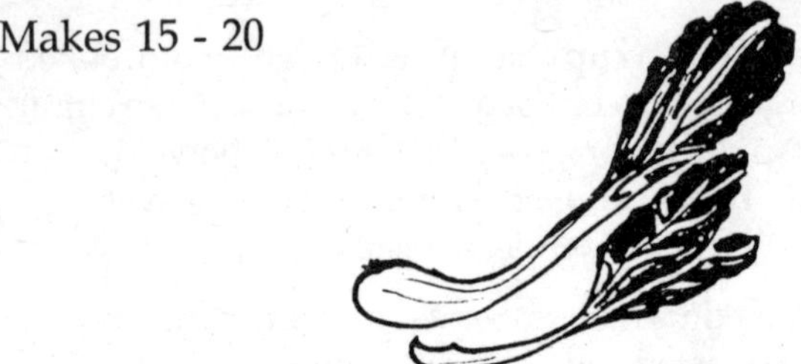

Satay (Barbecued meat) (Thailand)

All over Thailand you find vendors selling these succulent piece of meat kabab. You can use boneless chicken as well.

Ingredients

600 gm boneless meat cut into cubes. 1 clove of garlic. 6 small onions. ½ tsp pepper. 1 tbsp coriander pd. ½ tsp cumin pd. ½ tsp fennel pd. 1 tbsp sugar. salt to taste, lime sized ball of tamarind. 1 tbsp fish sauce.

Sauce : 1 large lime sized ball of tamarind. 12 small onions. 2.5 cm piece of ginger. 2 cloves of garlic. 1 stalk lemon grass. 2 tbsp refined oil. 2 cups thick coconut milk. 1 cup peasuts, coarsely ground. 1 tbsp fish sauce, salt, pepper and sugar to taste.

Parboil meat cubes; strain. Finely chop ginger and onions.

Soak tamarind in 4 tbsp hot water. Strain and remove pulp. Add the spices, ginger, garlic, onion, salt, sugar and fish sauce, marinate meat in it for 2 hours.

Thread onto skewers and barbecue or grill, rotating and basting with the marinade till done. Serve hot with the sauce.

Sauce : Grind the onion, ginger, garlic and lemon grass (white part only) together. Soak tamarind in 1½ cups of water. Extract juice.

Heat the oil in a saucepan. Saute the ground spices for 2-3 minutes. Add the coconut milk, peanuts, tamarind juice, fish sauce, salt, pepper and sugar to taste. Cook, stirring, continually over medium heat till thick. Remove.

Serves 6

Upside Down Meatloaf (U.K.)

Not only a comfort food, but sophisticated enough for any grown up party.

Ingredients

1 large tin pineapple, a few glace cherries and walnut halves. 500 gm finely minced meat. 2 tbsp Worcestershire sauce. ½ cup grated onion. ½ cup tomato ketchup. 1/3 cup fresh breadcrumbs. 2 eggs. salt and pepper to taste. 4 hardboiled eggs. handful of dry bread crumbs. 1 tbsp butter.

Grease an 8″ square baking dish and line with non-stick parchment paper, grease the paper too. Place the pineapple slices decoratively. Fill the gaps with walnut halves and the holes of the pineapple with glace cherries. Refrigerate till needed.

Mix all the remaining ingredients except the hardboiled eggs, breadcrumbs and butter. Place half the mince mixture over the pineapple in the dish. Place the eggs side by side. Cover with the rest of the mince. Sprinkle the breadcrumbs all over and dot with butter.

Bake in a preheated oven 200 °C / 400 °F for 50 minutes. Let cool for 10 minutes then invert on a plate. peel off the parchment paper. Cut in slices and serve with a salad. Tastes great cold, too.

Serves 4 - 6

Oven Fried Lemon Chicken (Continent)

This recipe is an all time favourite with my cookery classes.

Ingredients

1 chicken. ½ cup flour. salt and pepper to taste. 2 tsp Kashmiri chilli powder or ½ tsp chilli powder. 8 tbsp butter.

Sauce : 2 tsp soyabeen sauce. Salt and pepper to taste. ¼ cup groundnut oil. 1/3 cup lime juice. 1 tsp sugar. 2 tsp grated lime rind. 4 cloves of garlic, ground (optional).

Sauce : Combine all the ingredients. Mix well and refrigerate for one hour. Cut the chicken into serving sized pieces. Combine the flour, salt, pepper and chilli powder. Toss the chicken pieces in it.

Grease an ovenproof dish. Arrange the chicken pieces.

Spoon over the butter and bake in an oven preheated to 200 °C / 400 °F for 20 minutes.

Turn the chicken. Pour lime sauce over it. Bake for another 30 minutes or till done.

Serve hot.

Serves 4 - 6

Pearl Balls with Plum Sauce

The cooked rice adhere to the mince balls looking like pearls; hence the name.

Ingredients

200 gm rice. 300 gm minced chicken. 1 egg. 2 tsp finely chopped ginger. 2 tbsp cornflour. 2 tbsp soya sauce. 1 tbsp finely chopped spring onion. salt and pepper to taste. 1 tbsp groundnut oil. lettuce or tender cabbage leaves as needed.

Soak the rice overnight. Mix the rice with all the ingredients except lettuce leaves and rice.

Prepare lime sized balls from the mince mixture with wet hands. Drain the rice and coat the balls with it. Press very lightly so that the rice sticks to the balls.

Take a steamer and line it with the lettuce or cabbage leaves. Place the balls in it. Steam for 20 minutes, check once; steam for another 5 minutes, if necessary. Serve with plum sauce.

Plum sauce : ½ cup plum jam. ¼ cup sweet chutney. 1 tbsp vinegar. 1 tbsp sugar. Heat all the ingredients together over a low heat till the sugar dissolves. Cool and serve. Any other fruit jam may be used.

Serves 4

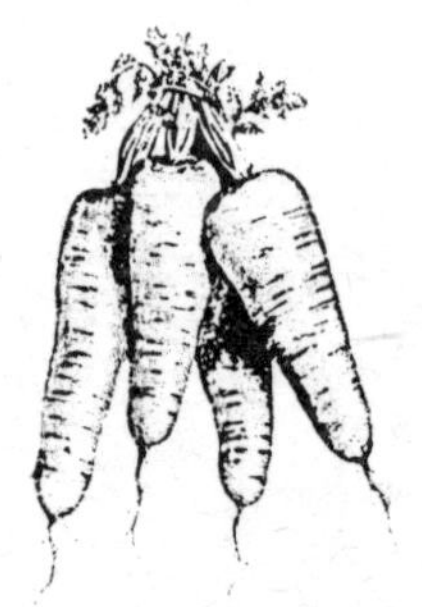

Doughnut

The size of the cutter. I have used is for small doughnuts. Serve them as snacks for children or at tea time. You can also prepare larger ones. They are generally served at breakfast.

Ingredients

250 gm flour. 1 tsp baking powder. 2 heaped tbsp butter. 120 gm sugar, powdered. 1 large egg. 4 tbsp milk. 1 tsp vanilla essence vegetable shortening for frying, icing sugar for dusting.

Sieve the flour and baking powder. Cream the butter and sugar till fluffy. Beat in the egg and vanilla. Mix the milk. Add the flour and mix to a dough. Place the dough on a floured surface and knead a few times. If it is too soft, refrigerate to haren. Do not add more flour. Roll it out to 7 mm thick. Use a small doughnut cutter 2 cm in diameter and cut the dough. Reknead the rest of the dough and cut again.

Heat enough vegetable shortening in a karahi and deep fry the doughnuts, a few at a time, till golden. Roll in icing sugar while still hot.

Serves 6

Variation : Instead of cutting make balls and stuff with half a teaspoon of jam. Coat the doughnuts with chocolate icing for chocolate doughnuts. You may omit 2 tbsp flour and add an equal amount of cocoa pd. to the dough.

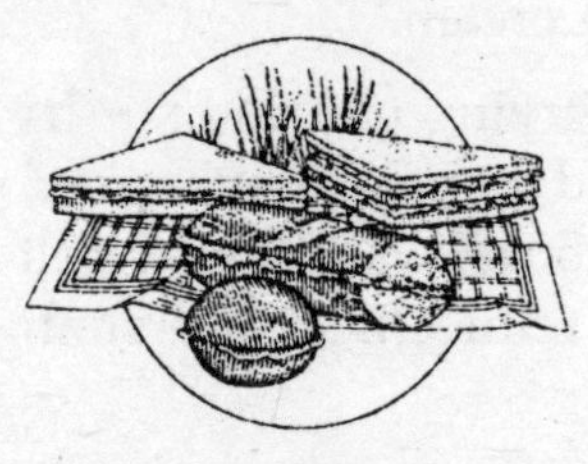

Meatballs with Satay Sauce (Malaysia)

This receipe is from the Nonya Cuisine. The federation of Malaysia is comprised of malay, chinese and Indian people. The housewives and professional chefs of Malaysia managed to retain their own authentic national styles of cooking, but have additionally secceeded in blending, those various styles to produce many new and exciting flavour of particular note is the Nonya cuisine, a style of cooking which is unique and virtually unknown outside Malaysia Singapore.

Ingredients

For the meat balls : ½ kg. minced meat. 1 medium onion, finely chopped. 1 clove garlic, crushed. 1½ cups fresh breadcrumbs. 1 egg. ½ tsp grated nutmeg. 2 tbsp chopped fresh coriander: 2 tbsp refined oil. Salt to taste.

Satay Sauce : 4 dried red chillis or to taste. 2 cloves garlic. 4 spring onions. 2 tbsp thick coconut cream. 50 ml refined oil. 150 gm peanuts. 2 tsp tamarind juice. 1 tbsp lime juice. 1½ tbsp sugar. salt and freshly ground pepper to taste.

Meatballs : Combine mince, onion, garlic, breadcrumbs, egg, nutmeg, coriander leaves and salt. Roll 2 teaspoons of mixture into balls.

Heat oil in a frying pan, add the meatballs and fry till browned and tender. Drain. Serve with Satay sauce.

Satay Sauce : Soak the chillis in water for an hour. Chop finely. Chop the garlic and spring onions. Grind all these with the coconut cream.

Heat the oil in a frying pan and stir fry the ground paste for 5 minutes. Add the coarsely chopped peanuts, tamarind juice, lime juice, 150 ml water, sugar, salt and pepper. Bring to the boil, then reduce heat and simmer until the sauce thickens.

Green chillis may be used in place of dry chillis.

Serves 4

Momo (Nepal)

Momos are steamed in a momo maker. It is a series of pans (about 3 -4) one on top of the other. The bottom one has water. The others have holes in the bottom to permit steam to go through to cook the momos which are kept in the upper pans. The topmost container is covered with a lid.

Ingredients

For the covering : 250 gm flour, little warm water.

For the stuffing : 250 gm minced meat. 2 tbsp refined oil. 250 gm spring onions. chopped with parts of the green tops. 3 tbsp thin soyabean sauce, green chillis, salt and pepper to taste. ¼ tsp monosodium glutamate (optional).

For the covering : Make a semi hard dough with the flour and warm water. Keep aside for 15 minutes, covered with a wet cloth. Divide into 24 parts. Roll into 2½ inch thin circles with the centre slightly thicker than the sides.

Place one portion of the stuffing in the centre of the disc and pinch or press the edges well together to make decorative boat shaped or walnut shaped momos.

Grease momo containers, place 8 momos in each pan and steam for 20 - 30 minutes or till done.

For the stuffing : The mince should have a some fat in it and must be very finely ground. Mix all the ingredients and set aside for 30 minutes. Instead of mince, chicken, prawn, vegetables or paneer, may be used.

Serve with the following momo sauce.

1 cup dry red chillis. 6 - 8 tbsp vinegar. 1 tbsp sugar. Salt to taste. Tomato ketchup, fresh coriander and lime juice to taste.

Remove the stems of the chillis. Discard the seeds of a few if you don't want the sauce too hot. Soak the chillis in hot water for 15 minutes.

Strain the chillis and grind to a paste with the vinegar, sugar and salt. Mix this paste with tomato ketchup, fresh coriander and lime juice to taste.

Not only momos, this sauce goes extremely well with any snack.

Serves 6

Cakes

Surprise Lime Cake

A delightful cake with a surprising crunchy filling and topping. Perfect for tea time or as a serumptious dessert.

Ingredients

100 gm flour. 50 gm rice flour. 1 tsp baking powder. 100 gm butter. 100 gm sugar, powdered, grated rind of 1 lime. 2 large eggs. Juice of 1 lime.

For the filling : 25 gm butter. 2 tbsp marmalade. 3 tbsp cornflakes sift the flour, rice flour and baking powder together.

Cream the butter and sugar in a large bowl till light and fluffy. Beat in the lime rind. Add the eggs one by one, beating after each addition.

Fold the flour mix gently into the butter and egg mixture, alongwith the lime juice.

Grease and paper line a 15 cm round cake tin. Grease the paper, too. Pour half the cake batter in the tin and smooth level. Place half the filling on top of this, then add remaining batter. Level surface.

Spoon remaining cornflakes on top evenly. Bake in preheated 350^0 F / 180^0 C oven for 1 hour and 10 minutes or until a skewer inserted into the centre comes out clean.

Filling : Melt the butter and marmalade together gently until smooth. Remove and stir in the cornflakes and mix well.

Banana Walnut Tea Bread

Treat yourself to afternoon tea in the garden and enjoy this tea bread cut into slices. Though called a bread, its more of a cake; but you can eat it spread with butter or honey.

Ingredients

1 cup flour. Pinch of salt. ½ tsp baking powder. 80 gm butter. 1 cup ground sugar. 2 egg yolks. 1 large ripe banana. 1 tbsp lime juice. ½ tsp vanilla essence. ¼ cup chopped walnuts. 2 egg whites.

Sift the flour, salt and baking powder together, Reserve. Mash the banana; add lime juice.

Cream the butter and sugar till light and fluffy. Beat in the egg yolks. One at a time. Stir in the mashed banana alongwith the vanilla.

Beat the egg whites separately till stiff. Fold the flour into the butter mixture alternately with the beaten egg whites. Lastly add the walnuts.

Grease and flour a ring mould. Pour in the batter and bake at 180^0 C for 30 minutes. Serve warm.

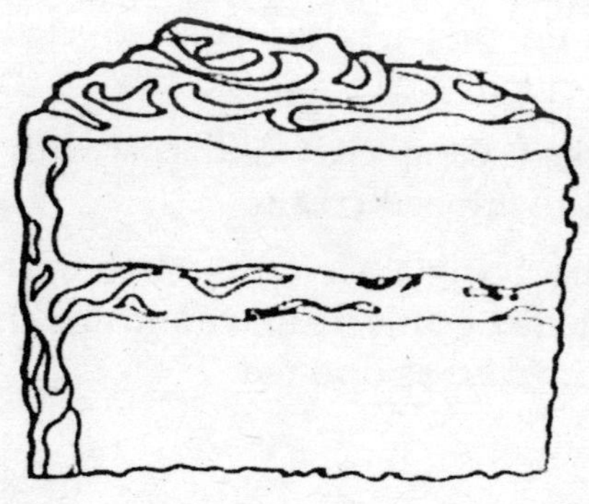

Sachertorte

Named after the Sachers, a family of Austrian hotel owners of the 19th and 20th century who created this rich chocolate cake.

Ingredients

100 gm walnuts. 100 gm butter. 125 gm castor sugar. 5 large eggs. separated. 1 tbsp rum. 75 gm chocolate chips or milk chocolate. 50 gm dry bread crumbs. ¼ tsp mixed powdered spice. Whipped cream for decoration.

Chocolate glace icing : 50 gm milk chocolate. 2 tbsp water. 1 tsp glycerine. 70 gm icing sugar.

Grease and line a 23 cm round cake tin with greaseproof paper; the side band should stand about 2 cm above the edge of the tin. Lightly roast the walnuts, then rub to remove the skin as much as possible. grind, to a powder. Cream together the butter and sugar until light and fluffy. Beat in the egg yolks, one at a time. Place the rum and chocolate chips in a basin over hot water and stir gently until melted, Fold into the butter mixture together with the nuts, crumbs and mixed spice.

Whisk the egg whites until stiff and fold in. Turn the mixture into the prepared tin. Bake at 400^0 F / 200^0 C for 30 minutes or until well risen and firm to the touch. cool.

When the cake is completely cold, coat with the icing and decorate with whipped cream.

To make the icing : Melt the chocolate, water and glycerine together gently. Remove and add the icing sugar. Stir till smooth. Use as directed.

Dundee Cake

A particular favourite of mine. A cake to have on hand all the time - if only you can.

Ingredients

185 gm butter at room temperature. 11/3 cups sugar. 6 eggs. ¼ cup orange juice. 2 cups currants or raisins. 1½ cups tutti fruitti. 1 cup chopped mixed peels. 2 tsp graped lime rind. 1 cup chopped blanched almonds. 3 cups flour. 1 tsp baking powder. ½ tsp salt. 1 tsp cinnamon. ½ tsp nutmeg. 12 whole blanched almonds for decoration. 1 tsp vanilla.

Cream the butter and sugar until light and fluffy. Beat in eggs, one at a time, beating well after each addition. Stir in the orange juice and vanilla essence.

Combine the currants or raisins, tutti fruitti. Candled peels, lemon ring and chopped almonds in a separate bowl.

Sift the flour and baking powder together. Add salt, cinnamon, and nutmeg and sift once more. Toss the dry fruits in it until they are well coated with flour.

Add to the creamed mixture and stir to blend. Spoon into a 23 cm round greased and paper lined tin.

Hollow out the centre a little so the cake rises evenly. Place the whole almonds decoratively on top.

Bake in a preheated 160⁰ C / 320⁰ F oven for about 1½ - 2 hours. This can be stored in an airtight container for a few days.

Raisin Nut Carrot Cake

Nutritions cake, made with oil instead of butter, full of goodness. Equally good for children and elderly persons.

Ingredients

2 cups flour. 1 tsp baking powder. 1 tsp bicarbonate of soda. 1 tsp ground cinnamon. 2 cups sugar powdered. 3 cups grated carrot. ½ cup raisins. ½ cup chopped walnuts. 1 cup refined oil. 4 eggs. 1 tsp vanilla essence.

Yogurt Frosting : 4 tbsp unsalted butter, softened. ½ cup hung curd. 2 cups icing sugar. 1 tsp vanilla essence.

Sift the flour, baking powder, soda and cinnamon together. Combine with the powdered sigar make a well in the centre and pour in the oil, eggs, carrots, raisins and walnuts. Beat with an electric beater at low speed till combined.

Grease and flour two 9" x 1½" round cake tin. Divide the batter equally between the two tins. Bake in oven preheated to 350° F / 180° C for 40 - 45 minutes or till done. Check after 40 minutes.

Beat together all the ingredients for the frosting till smooth. Spread over the slightly warm cake. The cake is very good without the frosting also.

Variation : Omit the raisins and nuts and bake or plain carrot cake.

Pineapple carrot cake : Omit raisin's and add 1 cup chopped pineapple and ¾ cup grated coconut.

Upside Down Gingerbread

Gingerbread is one of the most useful home bakes. It keeps well and cuts into neat slices. Have it for a packed lunch, tea or a supper snack. On a cold day try hot gingerbread with yogurt or custard for pudding.

Ingredients

Base : 1 tin pineapple. 6 walnut halves few glace cherries. 1 tbsp butter. 2 tbsp granulated sugar.

Cake : 50 gm golden syrup. 50 gm black treacle. 110 gm butter. 110 gm brown sugar a generous pinch of salt. 1 tbsp dry ginger powder. 170 gm flour. 150 ml milk. 1 tsp bicarbonate of soda. 1 egg. 1½ tsp cinnamon powder.

Base : Line a 17 cm square or round baking tin with greaseproof paper. Smear the butter and sprinkle sugar all over. Place the pineapple rings decoratively. Put the glace cherries, halved, in the cavity of the rings and cover the vacant places with walnuts. Refrigerate till needed.

Cake : Weigh the syrup and treacle straight into a pan (its easiest to weigh the pan and spoon and add the ingredients and spoon to the pan on the scales). Add the butter and sugar and stir them over a very gentle heat until the butter is melted.

Sift the salt, cinnamon and ginger into the flour. Mix well and make a hollow in the centre. Pour in the melted mixture.

Put the milk into the same pan and add the soda. Swirl it around, then add to the mixture with the eggs. Stir briskly to mix well. Pour in the prepared tin.

Bake in 320⁰ F / 160⁰ C preheated oven for 1 - 1¼ hours.

When ready it should be spongy in the centre and very slightly shrinking from the sides of the tin. Turn the cake up side down to cool, but leave the paper on until eating.

Variations : Baked without the topping, its plain gingerbread. Can be served warm with butter.

Hot ginger bread, cut into pieces and topped with whipped cream or custard makes a marvellous pudding.

Christmas Cake

You could ice this, of course. But a plain cake with a pretty coloured ribbon tied round it looks very gay and festive.

Ingredients

125 gm flour. ¼ tsp baking powder, pinch of salt. ¼ tsp mixed spice powder. 125 gm butter. 125 gm powdered sugar. 3 eggs. 250 gm dry fruits. 50 gm sugar for caramel.

Dry Fruits : 50 gm each of walnuts and cashewnuts, 25 gm each of sultanas, raisins, candied peels, crystallised ginger and tutti fruitti. Chop the nuts, peels and ginger.

Mixed Spices : 1 nutmeg. 2.5 cm stick of cinnamon. 5 cloves. 2 petals mace. Dry grind together. Keeps well in a bottle for at least 6 months.

Caramel Syrup : Put the sugar into a heavy bottomed pan with 1 tbsp water. Put on heat. The sugar will melt and then caramelise into a golden brown liquid. Remove from heat and pour 2 tbsp of water. Stir to dissolve Caramel. Be careful, it will splatter fiercely. Keep this aside.

Ideally, the fruits, peels nuts should be soaked in rum for at least a week prior to baking.

Line a deep baking tin with double thickness of greaseproof paper. Butter and flour the paper. Preheat the oven to 150^0 C / 300^0 F.

Sieve the flour, baking powder, salt and mixed spice together.

Take a large mixing bowl. Cream the butter and sugar till light and fluffy. Add eggs, one by one, beating well after each addition. Fold in the flour with a spatula, alternating with the caramel syrup. Stir in dry fruits and peels. Pour into the prepared tin and bake for 1½ hrs.

Rich Fruit Cake

It is a good idea to make a large cake and take it with you on holiday. It keeps well and is a good standby for any hungry member of the family.

Ingredients

30 gm candied peels. 50 gm petha. 50 gm crystallised fruits. 20 gm cashewnuts or almonds. 50 gm tutti fruitty. 50 gm raisins. ¼ cup rum, brandy or orange juice. 50 gm vegetable shortening. 50 gm white butter. 100 gm sugar, powdered. 3 eggs. 1 tbsp caramel syrup or golden syrup. 100 gm flour. ½ tsp spice powder.

Prepare a cake tin by lining with greaseproof paper. Grease and flour paper.

Chop the peels, petha, crystallised fruits, cashewnuts or blanched almonds. Soak them alongwith the tutti fruitty and raisins in rum or brandy for 7 days; add mixed spice powder now. If using orange juice, soak for 2 -3 days only.

Cream the butter, vegetable shortening and sugar together till light and fluffy. Add eggs one by one, beating well after each addition. Add caramel or golden syrup, now. Fold in the flour and fruits alternately.Pour into the prepared tin. Preheat oven to 150⁰ C / 300⁰ F; bake for 1 hour.

This cake also doubles up as an economical christmas cakes. It may also be covered with almond paste and decorated with royal icing.

Dark Sticky Gingerbread (England)

Gingerbread is one of the most useful home bakes. It keeps well and cuts into meat slices. Have it for a packed lunch, tea or snack. Hot gingerbread cut into squares and topped with whipped cream or custard makes a marvelous pudding.

Ingredients

50 ml golden syrup. 50 ml black treacle. 110 gm butter. 110 gm brown sugar a good pinch of salt. 1 tbsp ground ginger. 1½ tsp ground cinnamon. 1 tsp ground mixed spices. 170 gm flour. 150 ml milk. 1 tsp sodium bicarbonate.

1 egg grease and line an 18 cm baking tin weigh the syrup and treacle into a pan. Add the butter and sugar and stir over a very gentle heat until the butter is melted.

Sift the flour, salt, ginger and cinnamon together. Mix well and make a bay in the centre. Pour in the melted mixture. Pour the milk into the same pan and add the soda. Swirl it round, then add it to the mixture with the egg. Stir briskly to mix well, then pour in the tin. The batter will be quite runny.

Bake in an oven preheated to 325^{0}F / 160^{0}C for 1-1¼ hours. When ready, it should be spongy in the centre and very slightly shrinking from the sides of the tin. Turn the cake out to cool but leave the paper on until eating.

Desserts

Kimami Semai (Pakistan)

You need the fine quality of vermicelli for this dish.

Ingredients

1 kg sugar. ½ kg fine vermicelli, pinch of saffron. ½ cup ghee. ½ cup chopped nuts and raisins. 4 green cardamom. 4 cloves. 125 gm khoya, grated, silver leaf for garnishing.

Put the sugar and 1 Lt. water to boil. Stir till the sugar dissolves. Add saffron and cook over high heat for 10 minutes. In the meantime, heat the ghee and add the nuts and raisins, green cardamoms and cloves, bruised. Add the vermicelli, broken; fry till pink.

Add to the syrup alongwith the grated khoya. Stir over high heat till the water reaches the level of the vermicelli. Reduce heat and stir at times, till it is of halwa consistency. But the vermicelli threads should remain separate. Lastly add more dry fruits, if deserd and remove.

Serve warm or cold decorated with silver leaf and nuts.

Serves 10 - 12

Kiwi Fruit Gateau

A most decorative dessert from New Zealand. Kiwi fruits are easily available nowadays. Strawberries can be substituted.

Ingredients

For the choux pastry ring : 1 cup water. 125 gm butter. 1 cup flour. 3 eggs. 1 cup cold vanilla custard. 1½ cups cream, whipped with a little sugar and vanilla. 4 - 5 Kiwi fruit, peeled and sliced.

To make the choux ring : Put water and butter in a saucepan; stir until the butter melts, then bring to the boil. Add all the flour at once. Beat well with a spoon until the mixture leaves the sides of the pan and forms a smooth ball, about a minute. Remove at once.

Cool a little, then add the eggs, one at a time, beating well after each. The use of an electric beater helps. The mixture should look glossy and smooth.

Sprinkle a little water on a baking tray. Take about 2/3 of the pastry and shape into a circle 20 cm in diametre. Use damp fingers to press the pastry into shape. Pipe the rest of the pastry on the top edge of the circle. to make the sides of the gateau.

Bake in a preheated 220^0 C / 440^0 F oven for 15 minutes, then reduce heat to moderate -180^0 C / 350^0 F and bake for a further 30 - 40 minutes. The pastry should be golden brown and have no beads of moisture visible. cool.

Split the pastry shell through the centre and remove any soft mixture, if necessary spread custard on the bottom of the pastry then replace the top. Spread the whipped cream on top of the pastry, then arrange slices of Kiwi fruits over the cream. Refrigerate for an hour before serving.

Serves 8

Strawberry Pavlova

This superb dessert was name after the famed ballerina Anna Pavlova.

Ingredients

8 egg whites. Pinch salt. 2 cups castor sugar. 2/3 cups granulated sugar. 3 tbsp cornflour 3 tsp lime juice. 2½ cups cream, whipped. 15 - 20 strawberries, sliced.

Beat the egg whites with salt until soft peaks form, then add castor sugar, gradually, beat till stiff peaks form.

Combine the granulated sugar with cornflour and fold into the meringue mixture with lemon juice.

Drawn a 25 cm circle on non-stick baking parchment or aluminium foil; set on a baking tray.

Pile meringue mixture inside the circle and bake in a preheated 110°C / 220°F oven for 2 hours. Turn the heat off and let pavlova cool in the oven without opening the door.

Serve topped with whipped cream and sliced strawberries.

Serves 12

Crepes Suzette

The concept of wrapping a pancake around a filling of some kind and then eating it so that each bite has a bit of both is as universal as it is sheer common sense.

In France they have crepes - thin pancakes made from flour based batter which are wrapped around various fillings, savoury or sweet. The most famous being the classic dessert, crepes Suzette.

Ingredients

For the crepes : 1 cup flour. Pinch salt. 1 tsp grated lime rind. 2 eggs. 1½ cup milk. ¼ cup of water. 1 tbsp melted butter or refined oil for frying.

Orange filling : 50 gm butter. 50 gm caster sugar. grated rind and juice of 1 orange.

To make the crepes : Sieve the flour, salt and rind together. Make a well in the centre. Gradually beat in the eggs, milk and water until the batter is very smooth.

Heat 1 tsp oil in a non-stick frying pan. Tilt the pan so the oil coats the bottom and sides of the pan completely.

Pour in just enough batter to cover the base of the pan thinly and cook quickly until golden brown underneath. Turn and brown the other side, too.

Fill each crepe with orange mixture, fold in four. Remove from pan and keep warm.

When all the batter is used up, return filled crepes all together to pan, pour over a little brandy and ignite. When flame subsides, serve at once.

Orange filling : Cream the butter and sugar; beat in the orange juice and rind.

Serves 4

Mocha Fondue

Dessert fondues are a wonderful way to round off a meal. It is said that a restaurant in New York first served sweet fondues. Dessert fondues have gained immense popularity. I give below one idea. Use your imagination and make variations.

Ingredients

200 gm milk chocolate. ½ tbsp instant coffee powder. ¼ cups cream, fresh fruits, cake and biscuits for serving.

Grate chocolate and mix with coffee powder. Put the cream in fondue pot. Add the chocolate mixture and blend. Heat gently, stirring until smooth and blended.

The fresh fruits may include apple, peach, strawberry, mango, papaya, banana etc. all cut into bite sized pieces. The fruits should not be overripe.

Also serve cubes of butter cake, marshwallow, macaroon, sponge cakes etc.

Provide a plate and a long fondue fork for each guest.

Serves 4

Trifle Alaska

A pudding that's not to be trifled with its amazingly good.

Ingredients

3 tbsp vanilla custard powder. ½ Lt. milk. 3 tbsp sugar. 2 egg yolks. 1 ginger bread or jam filled swiss roll. 2 tbsp mixed fruit jam. 4 tbsp mango fruittee or any other fruit juice. 1 large tin fruit cocktail. 2 egg whites. 75 gm caster sugar. 2 tbsp desicated coconut.

Mix the custard powder with the milk. Whisk the sugar and egg yolks. Combine milk and egg yolk mix and cook over a low heat till the custard is of coating consistency, that is it should coat the back of the spoon. Remove and let cool. Keep covered so as to prevent a crust forming on the surface.

Slice the gingerbread or swiss roll and arrange in a straight side 1.75 Lt. oven proofdish.

Mix the jam, mango fruittee or juice, and 4 tbsp of the syrup from the can and stir over low heat till the jam melts. Pour over the cake and top with the drained fruit.

Pour the lukewarm custard over the fruit. Let cool for 10 minutes.

Whip the egg whites until it stands in soft peaks. Whisk in the caster sugar and descated coconut. Spoon the meringue over the custard. Press the back of the spoon lightly onto the meringue, then pull it away, to draw the meringue up into soft peaks.

Bake in preheated 180^0 C / 360^0 F oven 15 - 20 minutes, until the top is pale golden. Serve hot.

Serves 6

Mocha Pond Pudding

The pudding, when done has a spongelike texture on top and a sauce underneath; hence the name.

Ingredients

½ cup flour. ¼ cup sugar. 3 tbsp coco a powder. ¾ tsp baking powder. ¼ cup milk. 1 tbsp refined oil. ½ top vanilla essence. ¼ cup chopped walnuts. 1/3 cup sugar. 2 tsp instant coffee powder. ¾ cup boiling water.

Sift together the flour, sugar, 1 tbsp coco a powder and baking powder. Add the milk, oil and vanilla. Stir till smooth. Stir in the nuts. Transfer to an ovenproof casserole.

Combine 1/3 cup sugar, rest of the coco a powder, coffee powder. Gradually stir in the boiling water. Pour evenly over the batter. Do not mix any further.

Bake in preheated 350° F / 180° C oven for 30 minutes. Serve warm with chilled cream or ice cream, if desired.

Variation : Omit coffee powder, and it becomes brownie pond pudding.

Apple Pie

The saying goes as American as apple pie and that prove the nationality of this very good sweet dish.

Ingredients

500 gm apples. 50 gm butter. 3 tbsp sugar. 2 tbsp raisins.

For the sweet shortcut pastry : 100 gm butter. 70 gm caster sugar. 1 egg. ½ tsp vanilla. 175 gm flour. ½ tsp cinnamon powder. 4 tbsp cake crumbs.

Peel core and dice the apples. Place apples, butter sugar and raisins in a saucepan; cook over medium heat. Let cook for 3 - 4 minutes or till the apples are coated with butter sugar. Remove.

For the pastry : Cream the butter and sugar till light and fluffy. Add the eggs and vanilla and beat till mixed. Now, stir in the flour and mix to a dough lightly. Refrigerate for half an hour.

Take a 12 cm pie mould and line with 2/3 of the pastry with the help of your hands; raise the pastry so it covers the sides as well.

Mix the apple with cinnamon powder and cake crumbs. Spread over the pastry. Roll the remaining pastry with the help of a little flour to a thin circle. Cut into ribbons; cover the pie in a lattice like batter. Brush pastry with beaten egg.

Bake at 180° C / 360° F preheated oven for 50 - 60 minutes. The pastry should be golden brown and crisp. Brush with any fruit jam and serve hot with vanilla ice cream.

Serves 6 - 8

Almond Fruit Cream

Chinese cuisine does not boast of a large repertoire of desserts. But this one is most elegant and attractive. Serve in sherbet glasses and topp with a thin layer of fruit puree.

Ingredients

1 pkt. china grass or 1½ tbsp gelatine. 3 cups of water. 1 cup sugar. 1 cup milk. ½ tsp almond essence. 1 cup honeydew melon (kharbuja) pulp. 1 cup mango pulp.

Chop the china grass into pieces and soak in the water for an hour. Place in a saucepan and heat over a moderate heat. Make sure the china grass has melted completely, stirring with a spoon, as it comes to a boil. Add the sugar and stir until dissolved.

Pour in the milk and stir; as soon as the mixture comes to a boil, turn off the heat. Add the almond essence.

Allow the mixture to cool. But pour in the sherbet glasses while still quite warm. China grass sets at room temparature and must not be disturbed once it has started to set. The glass should be 2/3 full. Chill in the refrigerator once it has set.

Add 1 tbsp powdered sugar each to the fruit pulp. Pour the topping over the set jelly cream and serve.

If using gelatine, soak in ¼ cup of water and mix in the hot milk after the sugar has dissolved. Stir well and remove and proveed with the recipe. Gelatine sets only when refrigerated.

Serves 6

Ribbon Bavarois

A dessert from Southern Germany. This very rich, impressive mould makes an ideal dessert for a formal party. The time and trouble it takes to make it is well worth the final result.

Ingredients

2 tbsp gelatine. 6 tbsp water. 150 gm sugar. 2 tsp cornflour. 3 egg yolks, pinch of salt. 300 ml milk. ½ tsp vanilla essence, few drops strawberry essence and colour. 1 tbsp strong black brewed coffee. 1 cup thick whipped cream. 3 egg whites.

To decorate : 125 ml cream whipped with 3 tbsp sugar.

Soak the gelatine in the water for 15 minutes or till spongy. In a saucepan beat together the egg yolks, salt, cornflour and sugar. Slowly blend in the hot milk, stirring continuously. Cook over a slow heat until the mixture boils. Add the gelatine and remove. Stir till the gelatine dissolves completely.

Cool and then chill till partially set. Blend till smooth. Fold in the whipped cream. Separately beat the egg whites and fold gently but thoroughly.

Divide the mixture into three parts. To one part, add the strawberry colour and essence; to the second part, add the vanilla essence and to the last part, add the brewed coffee.

Grease a mould with oil. Place one part of bavarois in it and chill immediately. Then add the second part and chill. Finally top with the third part and chill for at least 6 - 8 hours.

Unmould and decorate with whipped cream. Serve cut in small wedges; because its a rich dessert a little goes a long way.

No Cook Cheese Cake

Here's your answer to 'what's for dessert' ? - When the weather's sizzling and the last thing you want to do is cook. Just fix this dessert without turning on the stove or oven.

Ingredients

20 cake rusks. 75 gm butter. ½ tsp ground all spice. 1½ tbsp gelatine. 3 egg yolks. 75 gm caster sugar. 1 cup hung curd. 1 cup soft paneer. ½ tsp vanilla essence. 2 tsp grated lime rind. 350 ml cream.

Crush the cake rusk to a coarse powder. Melt the butter and add the all spice and the cake crumbs. Mix well. Line the base of a 20 cm cake tin with a removable base with the rusk mix and place the tin the refrigerator for at least 30 minutes. Soak gelatine in ¼ cup of water.

Beat the egg yolks and sugar together in a bowl until pale and smooth. Cook over a double boiler for 5 minutes, stirring constantly. Add gelatine and stir till it completely dissolves. Remove from heat.

Beat the curd and paneer in the blender till smooth. Add the vanilla, and lime rind. Whip the cream till stiff peaks form and fold into the curd mixture.

Spoon this into the cake tin and chill for 4 hours or until set.

Remove the cake from the tin and place on a serving dish arrange any fruit or your choice decoratively on top and serve kiwi fruits and strawberries look particularly attractive.

Serves 6.

Brown Betty (U.S.A)

Once tasted, your guests will want more.

Ingredients

Crumb mix : 1½ cups thin arrowroot biscuit crumb.
1/3 cup melted butter.

Fruit Layer : 1¼ cup peeled and diced apple. 1¼ cup peeled and diced pineapple.

Seasoned Sugar : 3 cup browned sugar. 1 tsp cinnamon powder. ¼ tsp nutmeg powder. 1 tsp lime rind. 1 tsp vanilla essence. ½ tsp salt. Mix all together.

Lime juice mix : 2 tbsp lime juice. 6 tbsp water.

Dry fruit layer : ¼ cup raisins. ¼ cup chopped dates.

Finale : Mix the biscuit crumbs and butter together. Place 1/3 of the crumb mixture in a greased 8" (12 cm) pudding bowl. Top with ½ of the fruit layer. Sprinkle with half of the lime juice mix and half of the dry fruits. Cover the top with 1/3 of the crumb mix.

Repeat once more. Cover the bowl with aluminium foil. Bake in an oven preheated to 380⁰ F / 190⁰ C for 30 minutes. Uncover; let the pudding brown on top for 10 minutes.

Serve warm with ice cream.

Serves 6

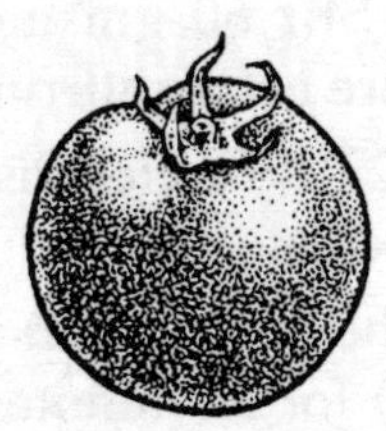

Burnt Coffee Custard (U.K.)

A more sophisticated version of the caramel custard. The added coffee and liqueir gives the custard a slightly darker colour and a delicious flavour.

Ingredients

250 gm sugar. 8 eggs. 1 Lt milk. 150 ml strong coffee. 3 tbsp coffee liqueer or brandy.

Put 100 gm sugar into a saucepan with ¼ cup of water and stir over a low heat till the sugar dissolves. Stop stirring and bring the mixture to a boil. Boil steadily till it caramelises. Pour into a ring mould, turning it so the base and sides are coated with the caramel.

Whisk the eggs and the remaining sugar together till well mixed scald the milk and pour in the coffee and stir well. Mix with the egg when lukewarm. Add the coffee liqueir or brandy and strain into the caramel lined mould.

Bake in a water bath; this means put the mould in another baking tin containing hot water. Cover the mould with foil and bake in an oven preheated to 325^0 F / 160^0 C for 1¼ hours or till set.

Remove from the oven and leave to cool completely. Chill overnight to turn out custard, place mould on the table and put a deepish serving dish over it. Hold the dish and mould together and turn them over. Lift the mould carefully. Serve with whipped cream or ice cream.

The custard can also be baked in individual small bowls.

Miscellenious

Brinjal Eggah

Cooking of Lebanon with its emphasis on curd and spices is quite similar to Indian cooking. Its a wonderful cuisine - spicy but not hot, rich in flavour, but generally low in fat.

Ingredients

1 large brinjal. 4 - 5 springs parsley, 2 stalks spring onion.
Salt and freshly ground pepper to taste. 1 tbsp lime juice.
6 eggs, separated. 1 tbsp refined oil.

Very finely chop the parsley and spring onion, with some of the green parts. Roast the brinjal over gas or in an oven till soft and the skin blackened. Peel and chop the flesh finely. Mix with salt, lime juice, parsley and spring onion.

Beat the egg yolks adding a pinch of salt and pepper. Mix with the brinjal.

Separately beat the egg whites till stiff (make sure your bowl and beater are scrupulously clean). Carefully fold into the brinjal with a very light hand.

Grease a baking dish generously with the oil. Pour in the brinjal mixture. Bake in an oven preheated to 350^0 F / 180^0 C for 45 minutes.

This eggah rises like a souffle. Serve at once. But unlike a souffle this tastes good eater eaten warm or cold.

Serves 6

Chilli Eggs

In the kitchens of Singapore, where truly East meets East, the many styles of Chinese cooking compete with richly spiced foods of the Indians, Malays and Indonesians. Here a multitude of cooks manage not only to successfully reproduce the traditional fare but also to create new and exciting recipes by blending cuisines like elsewhere people blend spices.

Ingredients

6 hardboiled eggs. 4 - 6 green chillis. 2 cm ginger. 2 cloves garlic. 3 tbsp refined oil. 1 tbsp sugar. Salt to taste. Freshly ground pepper to taste. Pinch monosodium glutamate. 300 ml chicken stock. 2 tsp vinegar. 2 tsp light soya sauce. 1 egg. 1½ tbsp tomato ketchup.

Chop the green chillis, ginger and garlic. Heat the oil in a Karahi and fry the hardboiled eggs till lightly coloured. Remove.

Add the chilli, ginger and garlic to the oil and saute till aromatic about 1 - 2 minutes. Add sugar, salt, pepper and monosodium glutamate and pour in the stock. Bring to the boil and add the eggs. Cook over medium heat for 5 - 7 minutes or until the gravy is reduced to half.

Add the vinegar, soya sauce and tomato ketchup. Beat the eggs lightly and add to the sauce and stir for a further minute until the egg begins to set and the sauce thickens slightly; serve with bread.

Serves 6

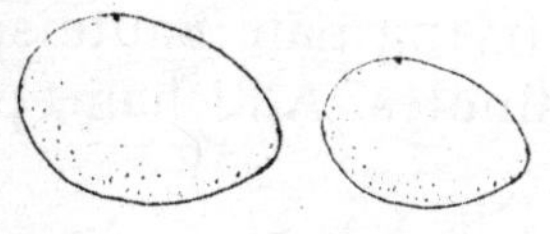

Green Tomato Chutney

Goes well with any meal - continental or even Indian.

Ingredients

3 large cooking apples. 1.5 kg green tomatoes. 500 gm onions. 1 cup raisins. 2 cups malt vinegar. 4 cups brown sugar or more to taste 6 cloves. ½ tsp dry ginger powder. 1 tsp white pepper. ½ tsp chilli powder. 1/3 cup mustard seeds. 1 tbsp salt. 1 bay leaf.

Peel, core and chop the apples. Cut tomatoes into quarters. Roughly chopped onions.

Place in a stainless steel saucepan or degchi. Add the raisins or mix well. Add vinegar. Bring to boil, stirring continually. Cover and simmer for one hour, stirring in between.

Add the sugar, cloves, ginger, pepper, chilli, mustard seeds, salt and bay leaf - simmer gently uncovered, stirring for another 1½ hours. The chutney should be thick and smooth. The vinegar should have evaporated.

Pour into hot sterilised jar. Seal well. This chutney will keep for months and will mellow with storage.

Sweet Sour Prawn Mango Pickle
(Bangladesh)

Will keep for a long time, if you manage to hide the bottle well.

Ingredients

2 onions. 2.5 cm piece of ginger. 8 cloves of garlic. 2 cups grated raw mango. 1 cup mustard oil. 2 tsp chilli pd. 1 tsp turmeric. 1 spring curry leaves. salt to taste. 2 cups shelled and deveined prawns. 1 cup sugar. 12 peppercorns. 2 tsp vinegar. 10 green chillis. 2 tsp mustard pd.

Grind the onions, ginger and garlic together.

Heat the oil in a Karahi. Add the ground paste, chilli pd., turmeric, mustard pd., curry leaves and salt. Fry for 10 minutes on medium heat.

Add the grated mango (squeeze mango to get rid of extra juice), prawns, sugar, peppercorns, vinegar and slit green chillis. Keep stirring till the moisture evaporates.

Cool and bottle.

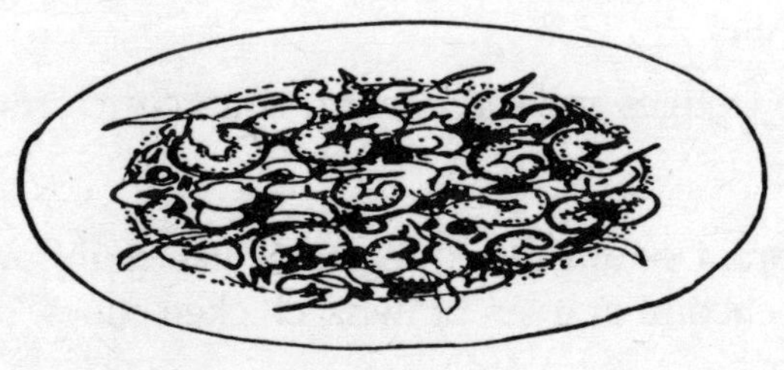

Frittata

A frittata is a type of Italian omelette - thick with a variety of vegetables, fish or meat. You can add almost anything to the eggs. It is also delicious eaten cold and makes an ideal picnic or travel food.

Ingredients

4 tbsp refined oil. 1 large onion, chopped. 2 cloves garlic, chopped. 250 gm broccoli, sliced thinly and blanched. 4 eggs. 1½ cup cooked peas. 3 tomatoes, blanched, peeled, seeded and chopped. 2 tbsp parsley. 1 tbsp fresh basil. 2 cubes cheese, grated. salt and pepper to taste.

Heat 2 tbsp oil in a frying pan and sante and onion and garlic till soft and transfucent. Add the broccoli and cook for 3 - 4 minutes.

Beat the eggs into a bowl and add the salt and pepper, onion mix, peas, tomato, parsley and basil.

Heat the remaining oil in a 24 cm skillet. Add the egg mixture and fry gently for 7 - 8 minutes or until the eggs have almost set and the underneath is brown.

Sprinkle the cheese over the top and place the pan under. Grill for 3 - 4 minutes or until set on top but still moist in the middle.

Cut into wedges and serve warm or at room termperature.

Serves 4

Variation : Use any other vegetable like cauliflower, baby corn, zuchchini or even prawns, chicken cubes, or minced meat.

Bevarages

Hawaiian Iced Coffee

Ingredients

1½ tbsp instant coffee. 2 tbsp sugar. 3 cups coffee ice cream. 1 cup chilled orange juice. 6 tbsp chocolate syrup.

Prepare coffee with 2 cups of milk. Dissolve the sugar in it. Chill.

Mix the coffee, ice cream and orange juice till smooth.

Serve in tall glasses drizzled with chocolate syrup.

Serves 4

Daylight Glory

Ingredients

2 ripe peaches, peeled and stored, 100 gm strawberries. 1 tbsp lime juice cordial. 300 ml sweet lime juice. 300 ml apple juice 1 Lt. lemonade. 10 sweet lime slices.

Blend the peach and strawberries with the lime and sweet lime juice. Strain into a jug.

Stir in the apple juice and top with lemonade.

Serve on crushed ice. Decorate the rim of each glass with a slice of sweet lime.

Serves 10

Banana Smoothie

This drink will revive the most jaded palate.

Ingredients

1 apple. 1 banana. 2 cups orange juice. 1 tbsp lime juice. Powdered sugar to taste. Pinch black salt. Pinch pepper powder. Lots of crushed ice.

Peel and chop the apple and banana. Blend in the mixer with the remaining ingredients till smooth.

Divide equally between 2 tall glasses. Top with crushed ice. Decorate with apple peel and a cocktail umbrella.

If you find it too thick, thin down with a little chilled water.

Red Indian

Toast summer with a glass of this mocktail.

Ingredients

1 cup blanched, deseeded and chopped tomatoes. ¼ cup orange squash. 1 tbsp sugar. 1 tsp black salt. ¼ tsp pepper. Lots of crushed ice.

Blend all ingredients together except the ice.

Pour in a highball glass. Top with crushed ice.

Decorate with finely chopped apples and orange slices.

Serve 1